Guide to Men's Tailoring

Volume 1

How to make shirts, trousers and vests

Guide to Men's Tailoring
Volume 1
How to make shirts, trousers and vests

Sven Jungclaus

Bibliografische Information der Deutschen Nationalbibliothek:
Die Deutsche Nationalbibliothek verzeichnet diese Publikation
in der Deutschen Nationalbibliografie; detaillierte bibliografische
Daten sind im Internet über www.dnb.de abrufbar.

2nd edition
© 2025 Sven Jungclaus
Cover: Michael Punz
Pictures: Wolf Silveri
Pictures extras: Sven Jungclaus

Publisher:

BoD · Books on Demand GmbH, Überseering 33,
22297 Hamburg, bod@bod.de
Print:
Libri Plureos GmbH, Friedensallee 273, 22763 Hamburg
ISBN: 978-3-8192-7880-8

Link to the
shirt videos

https://www.becomeatailor.com/videos-shirt/

Link to the
trousers videos

https://www.becomeatailor.com/videos-trousers/

Link to the
waistcoat videos

https://www.becomeatailor.com/videos-waistcoat/

It all starts here ...

Bespoke tailoring is not just sewing and nothing for beginners. On the other hand, at some point, everybody started. The important thing is not to be afraid of undoing a seam and preserving patience and perseverance. In between, you can almost despair that nothing works as you would like. But the knot comes off at some point, and you wonder why it took so long. Tailoring is about something other than being exceptionally fast. It is more important to work very neatly and accurately. The speed then comes by itself.

Practice creates masters
Especially at the beginning, you should not be satisfied with average results but always try to improve. A tailor's apprentice does hundreds of buttonholes, piping pockets, and more until they become even, tidy, and perfect.

Train your hands and eyes
With each pocket and each buttonhole, you gain more skills. The eye can then recognize the difference between 4 and 5 mm. Finally, the hands and eyes have to be trained for this craft.

A craft is not learned in an afternoon
You should take your time for tailoring. Sewing something in between can work, but it usually looks like this. Especially at the beginning, you always have to keep the goal in mind, and like chess, you have to think several steps in advance because every action has a consequence. And if you notice the error after five more steps, the correction is even more troublesome.

First think, then start
Each chapter has countless steps, and their order is significant for success.
Therefore, it is essential for the first sewing attempts to deal with the topic, read the whole chapter, think about it, and, if necessary, reread it until you have understood it theoretically.
Our videos are designed to help you carry out the steps in an orderly manner. Before each chapter, there is a link that leads to the instructions.
Only then it does make sense to venture into practice. Otherwise, you can easily overlook something, forget it and, in the end, almost despair because everything has to be taken apart again.

Just do not lose heart
Anyone who has specific motor skills can tailor. You just have to start; the rest comes with repetition.

Have fun, endurance and patience while tailoring!

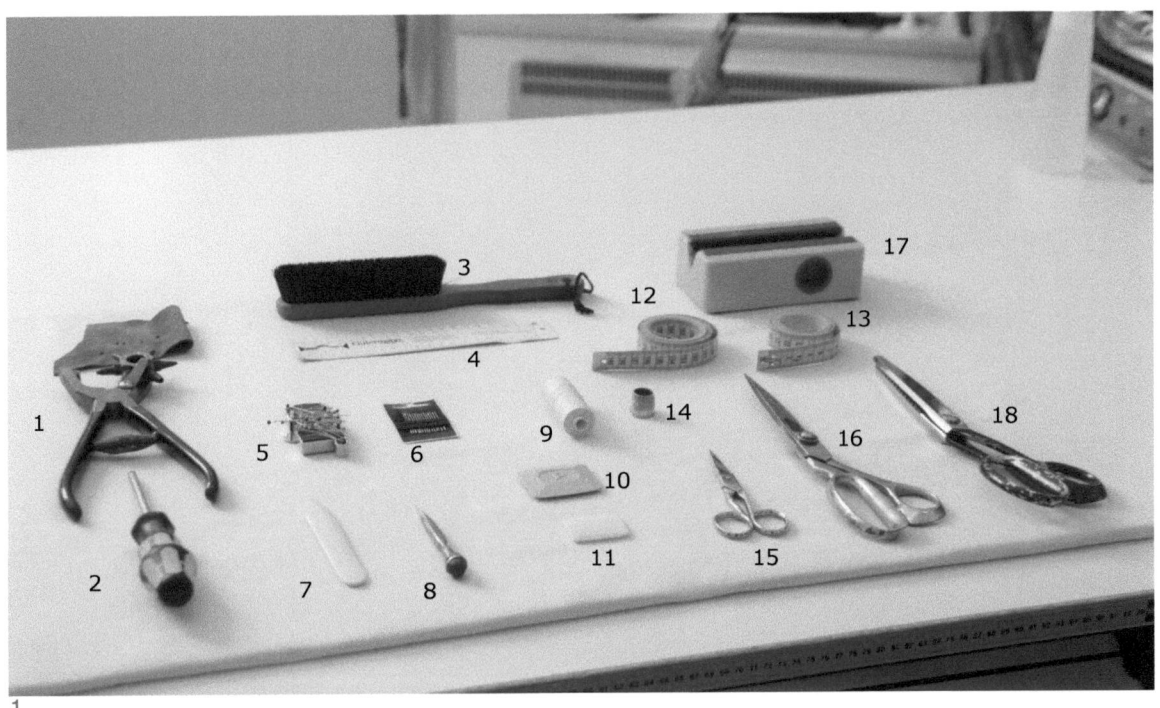

1

Sewing tools

1 Buttonhole spring punch
2 Phillips screwdriver
3 Clothes brush
4 Gauge
5 Pins
6 Sewing needles
7 Bonefolder
8 Awl
9 Basting thread

10 French chalk
11 Sublimating chalk
12 Tape measure
13 Waist tape measure
14 Thimble
15 Scissors
16 Shears
17 Chalk sharpener
18 Pinking shears

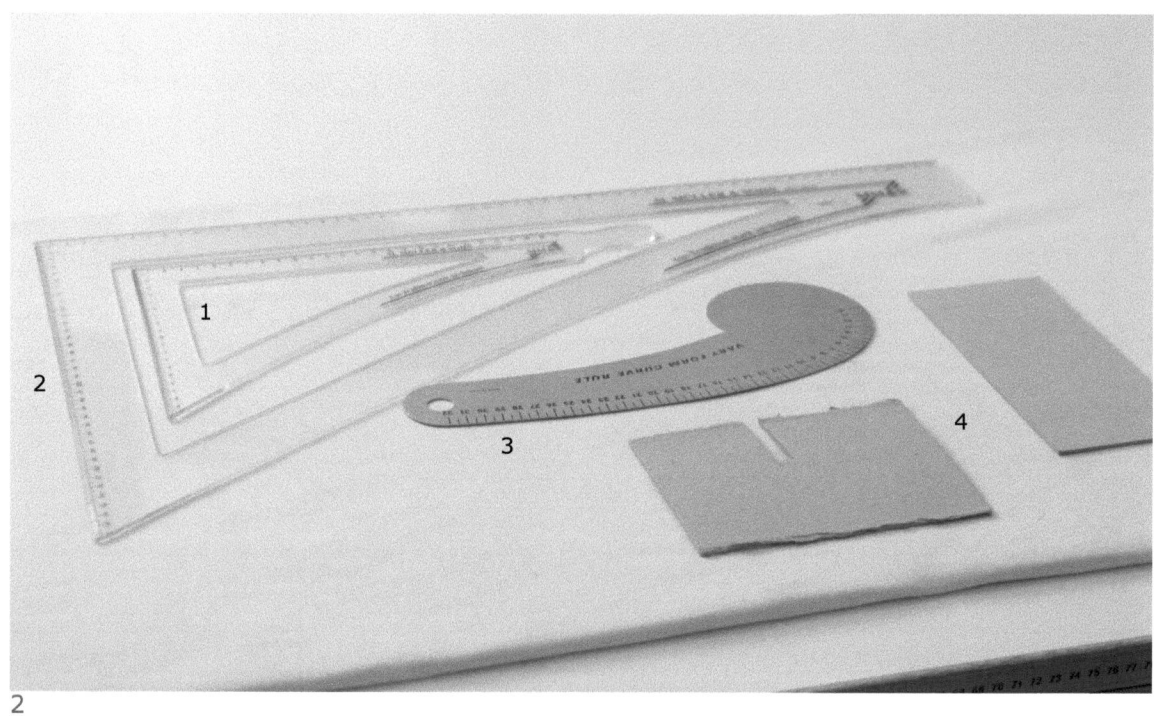

2

Useful tools

1 Small french curve
2 Big french curve
3 Armhole template

4 various cardboard templates
  according to your needs

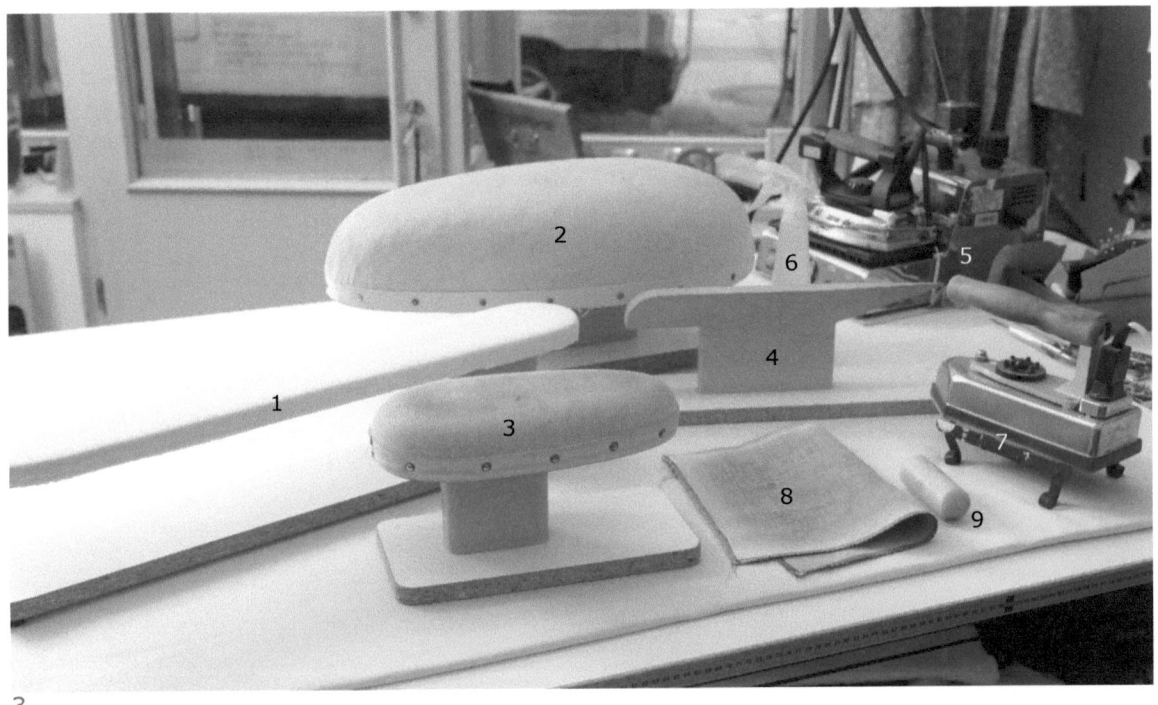

3

The ironing tools

1 Sleeve board

2 Torso pressing pad

3 Shoulder pressing pad

4 Ironing board for edges / clapper

5 Steam iron
   (Battistella Vaporino Inox Maxi)

6 Spray bottle

7 Heavy dry iron

8 Ironing cloth

9 Beeswax

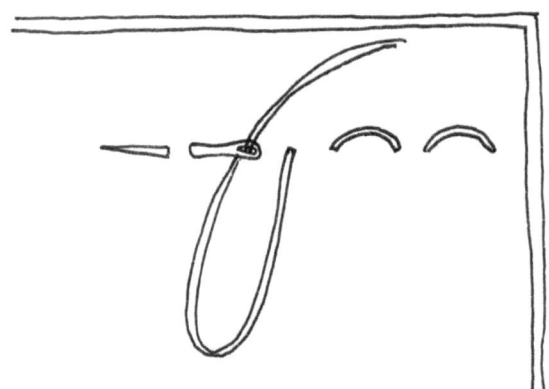

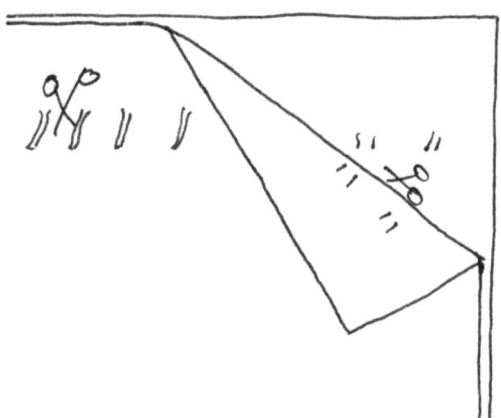

Tailor tacking part 1

This transfers the chalk marks to the right side of the fabric and the other piece of cloth. First, loosely pinch with a double thread and cut open the stitches.

Tailor tacking part 2

Then carefully cut between the pieces of cloth. At the end, cut off the protruding threads. See also tacking the vest (p. 80).

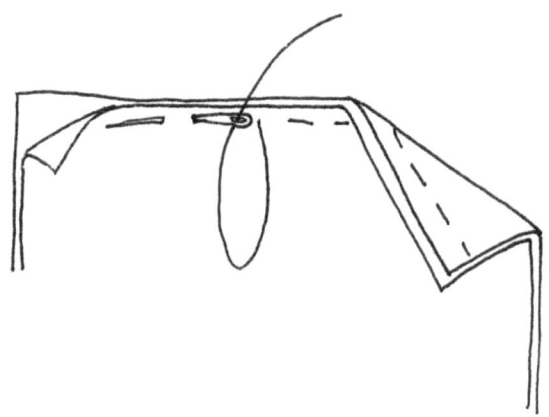

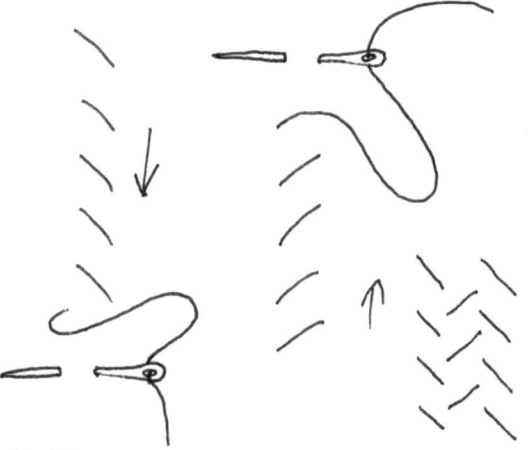

Basting

For a quick connection, fixing and securing of 2 or more layers of cloth.

Pad stitching

For a permanent connection of 2 or more layers of cloth and canvas. Mainly used for the canvas itself (horsehair), under collars and lapels.

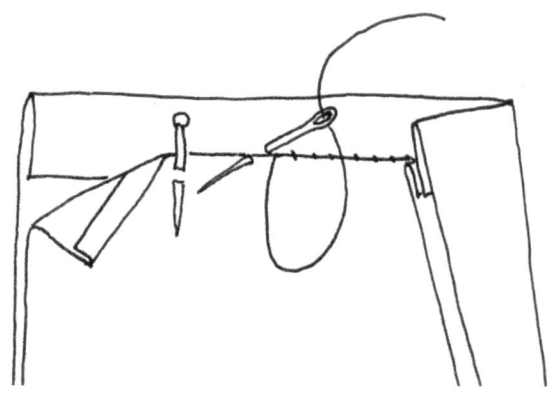

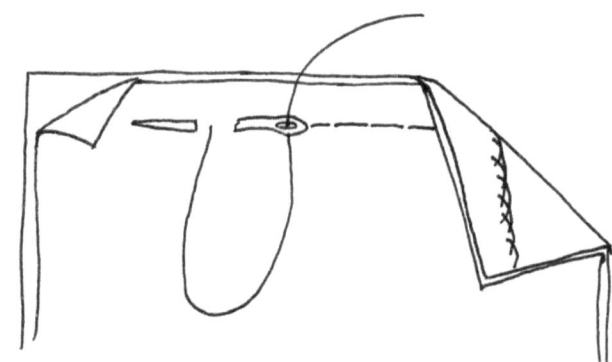

Blind stitching

For sewing in the lining. But it can also be useful in other places.

Backstitch

For elastic seams such, e.g. the buttocks seam. But can also be used for all other seams, if you want to do it without the sewing machine.

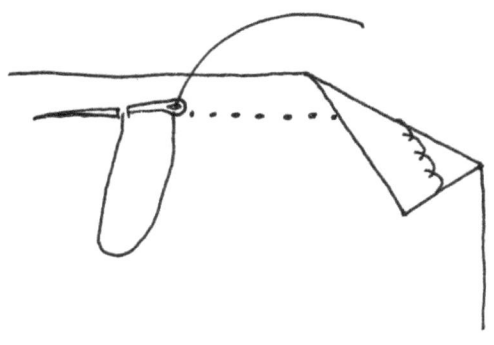

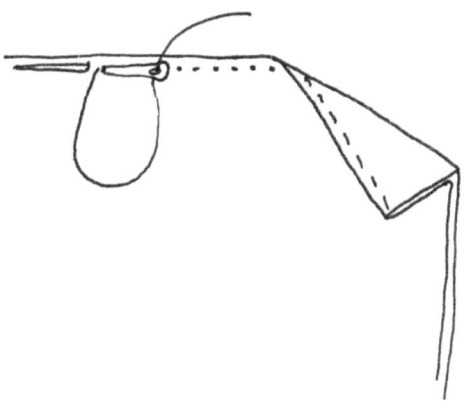

Prick stitch
Is often used as decorative stitching for sewing in the lining. Unlike sink stitching, a nodule should be visible.

Quick sinking stitch
For places that are not obvious, such as, e.g. hem edges and back vents.
(see page 102, picture 328)

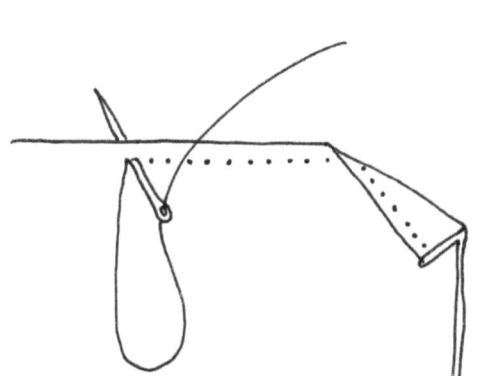

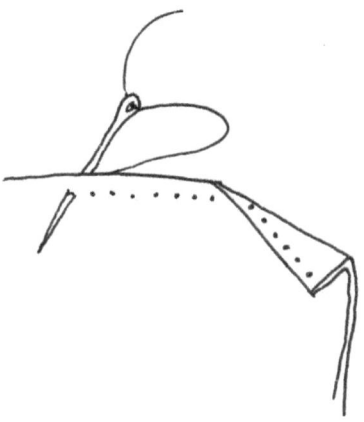

Carefully sewn sinking stitch part 1
For edges, lapels, flaps and other things, so that they remain flat and do not swell due to moisture.

Carefully sewn sinking stitch part 2
This variant is a bit more elaborate but gives a lovely stitch pattern on both sides. (see page 102, pictures 329/330.)

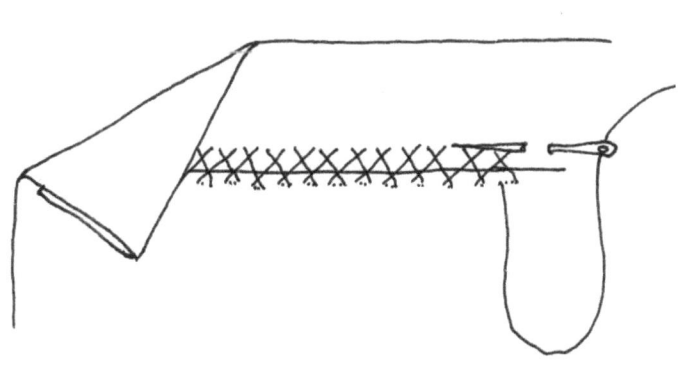

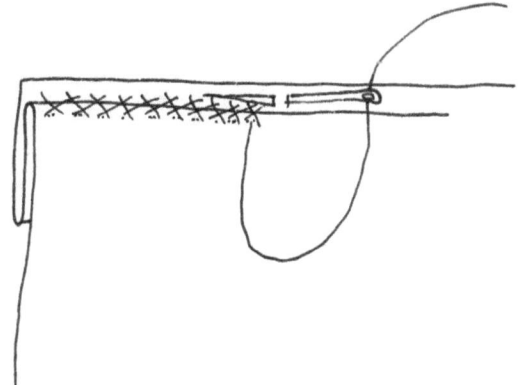

Cross stitch
This stitch is not used very often but still is very important in some places.

Hemstitch
As the name indicates, it is suitable for fixing hems. Unlike the cross-stitch, the seam allowance is not visible on the right side when ironing flat.

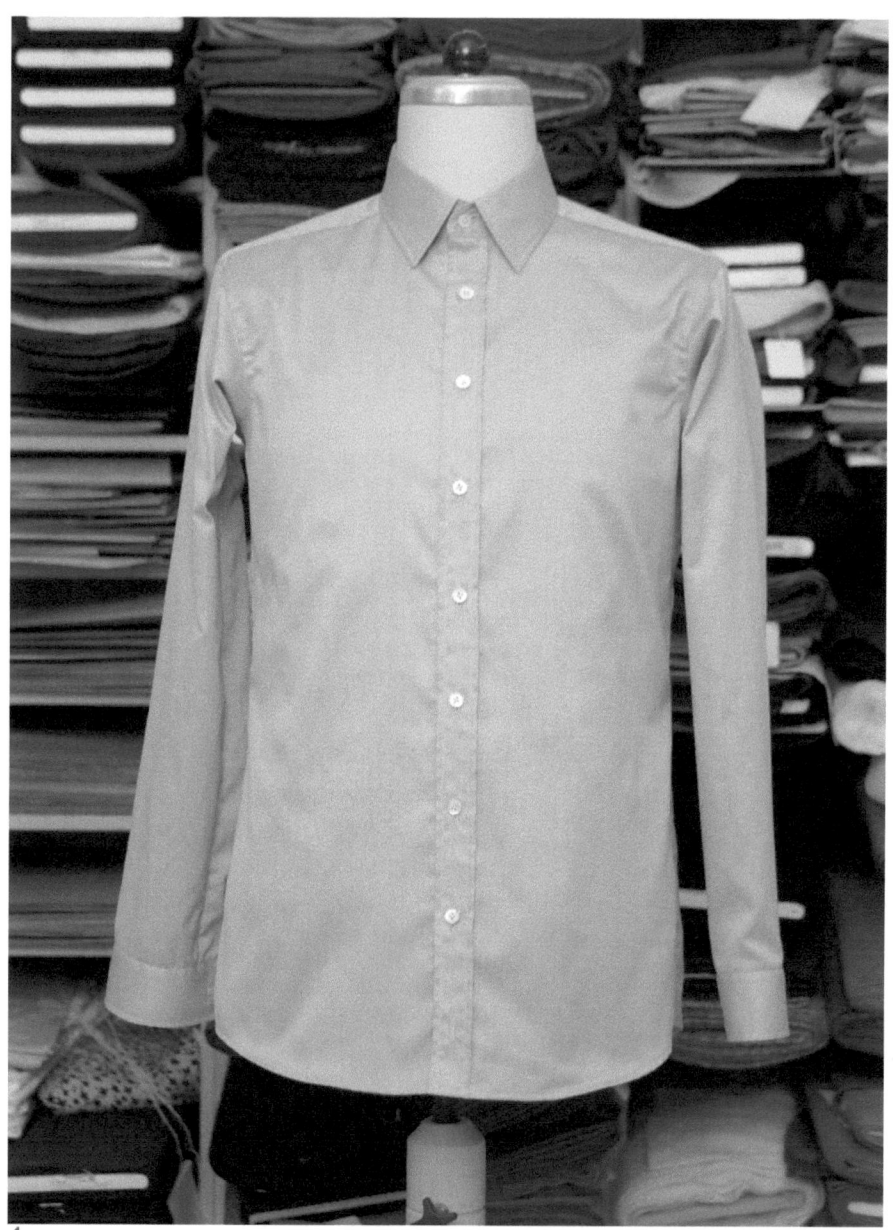

4

Link to the
shirt videos

https://www.becomeatailor.com/videos-shirt/

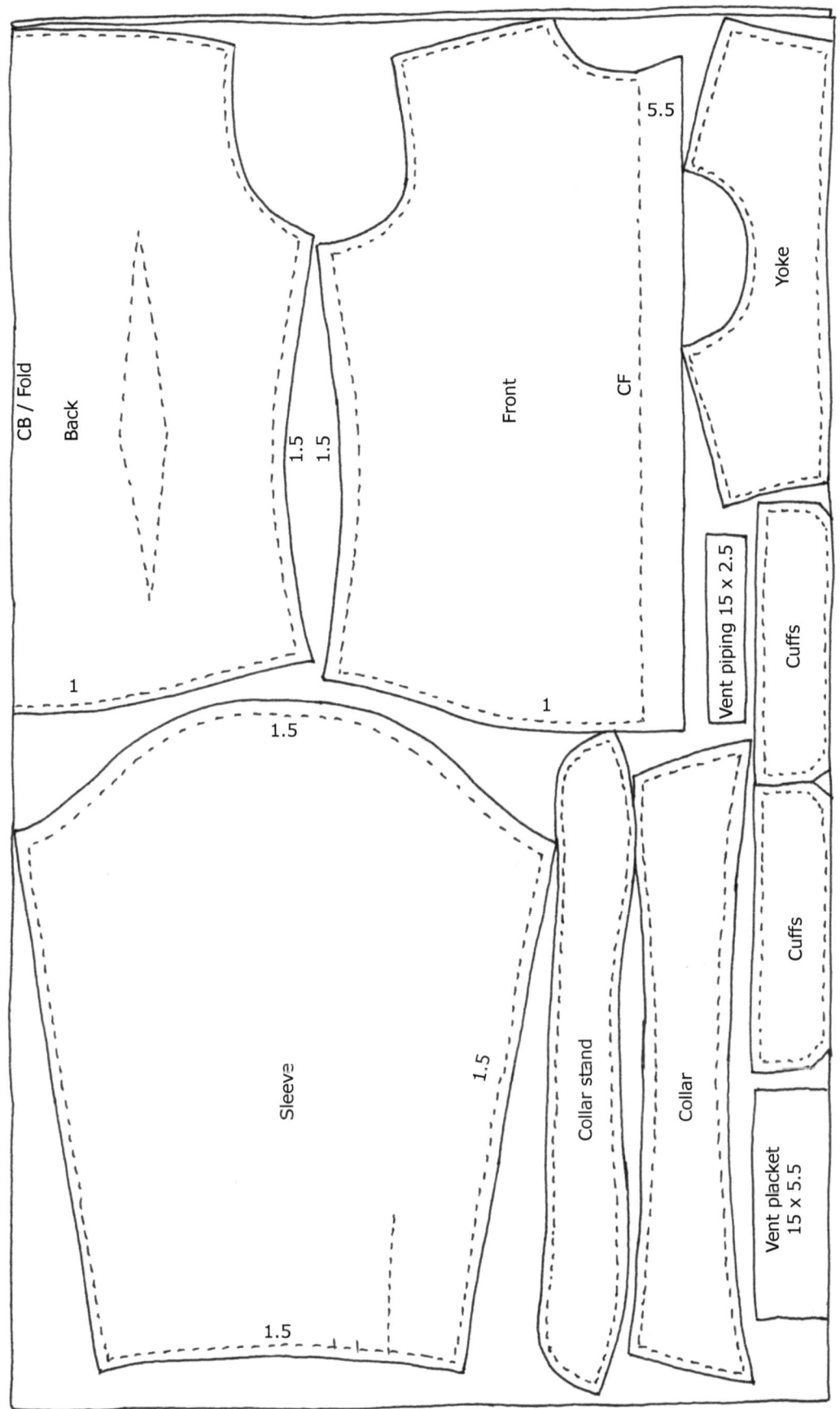

Cutting the shirt

Before cutting, it is essential to wash the fabric - which is usually made of cotton or linen - in the washing machine with the gentle or wool program at 30° C. The fabric can shrink significantly. With prewashing, the collar fits even after processing and when the shirt will be rewashed.

The seam allowances are marked as indicated in the drawing. Otherwise, at least the seam allowance of 0.75 or 1 cm is marked everywhere (see also explanation on page 127).

The shirt

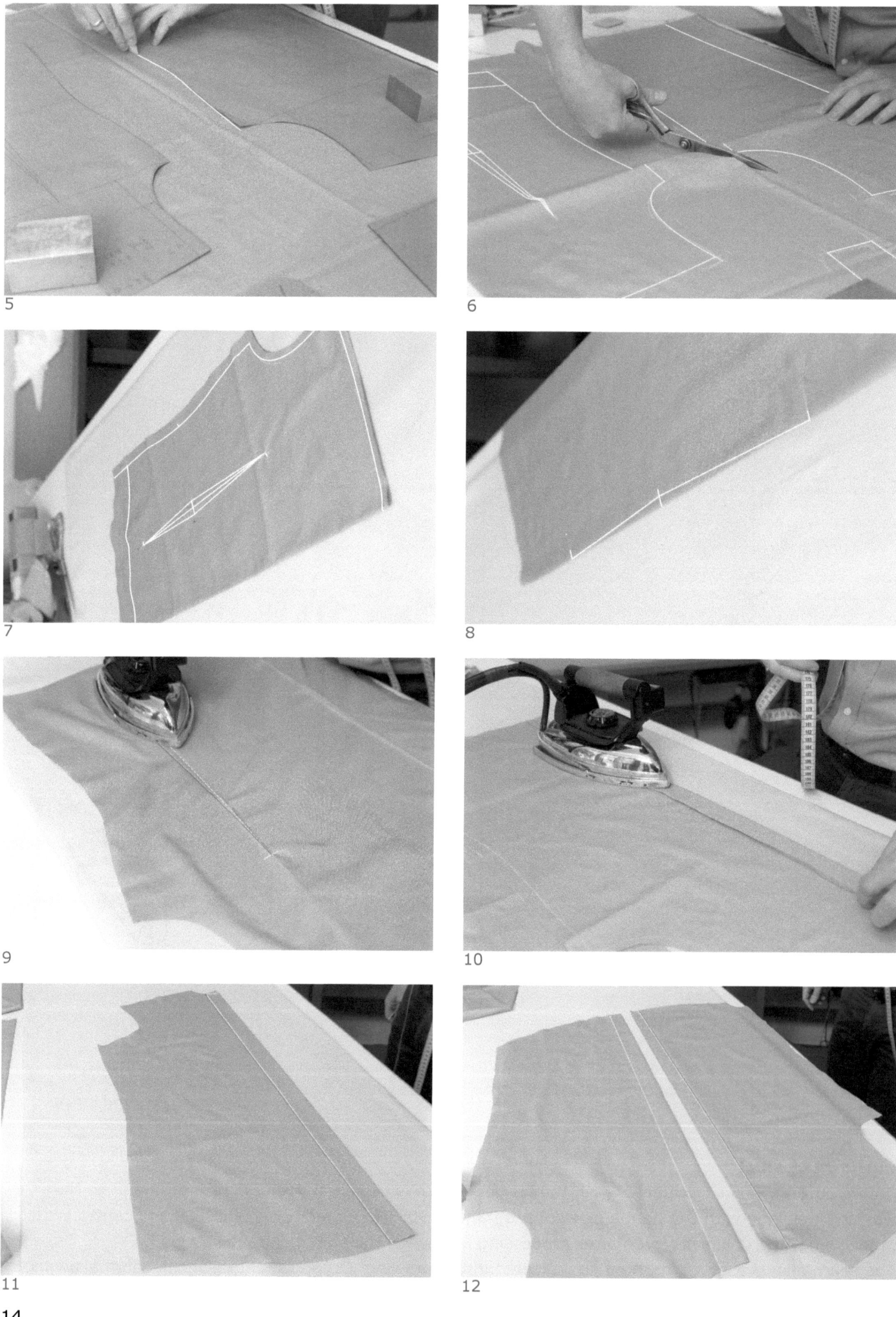

5

6

7

8

9

10

11

12

The cutting

Pictures 5/6

When cutting the shirt, you do not necessarily have to pay attention to the threading unless you work with corduroy, flannel or something similar.

For white fabrics, drawing the cutting parts carefully with a thin, soft pencil is advisable. These marks will be removed with the next washing.

The back darts

Picture 7

With pins, the dart is transferred and retraced to the other side.

Picture 8

Then, the darts are folded at the dart-center-line and pressed.

Picture 9

When stitching, the seam must be locked at the beginning and the end (sewing back and forth). After that, the darts are ironed flat toward the side seam.

The lower flap

Picture 10

The edge of the right front part - the lower flap/ bracket - is first folded by 1 cm and ironed flat, then folded by 3 cm and ironed flat to the wrong side of the fabric.

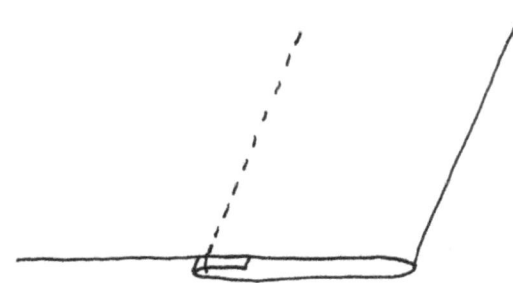

A strip of adhesive interlining can be added inside to reinforce the lower flap for holding the buttons. Now, the lower flap is sewn from the back very narrow to the edge (about 1 - 2 mm).

The button bar

Picture 11

The edge of the left front piece, the button bar, is folded and ironed twice by 3 cm. The cutting edge has to lie precisely in the fold. A strip of adhesive interlining can be added inside to reinforce the button bar.

Then, the edge is stitched by approx. 5 mm.

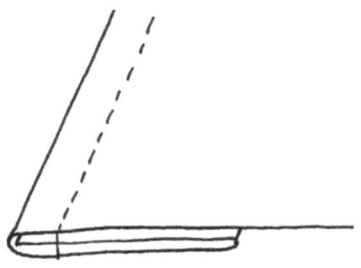

After that, the front part is folded back and ironed flat.

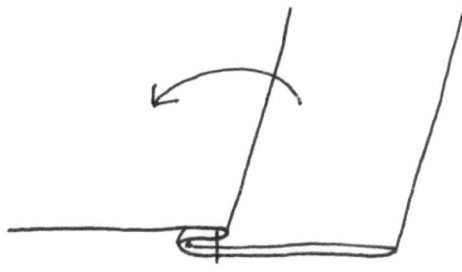

For symmetry, stitch the button bar on the other side by approximately 5 mm.

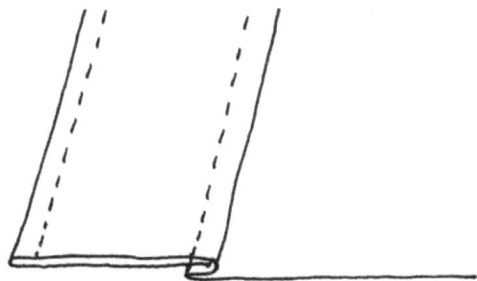

Picture 12

Left and right finished edges placed side by side.

15

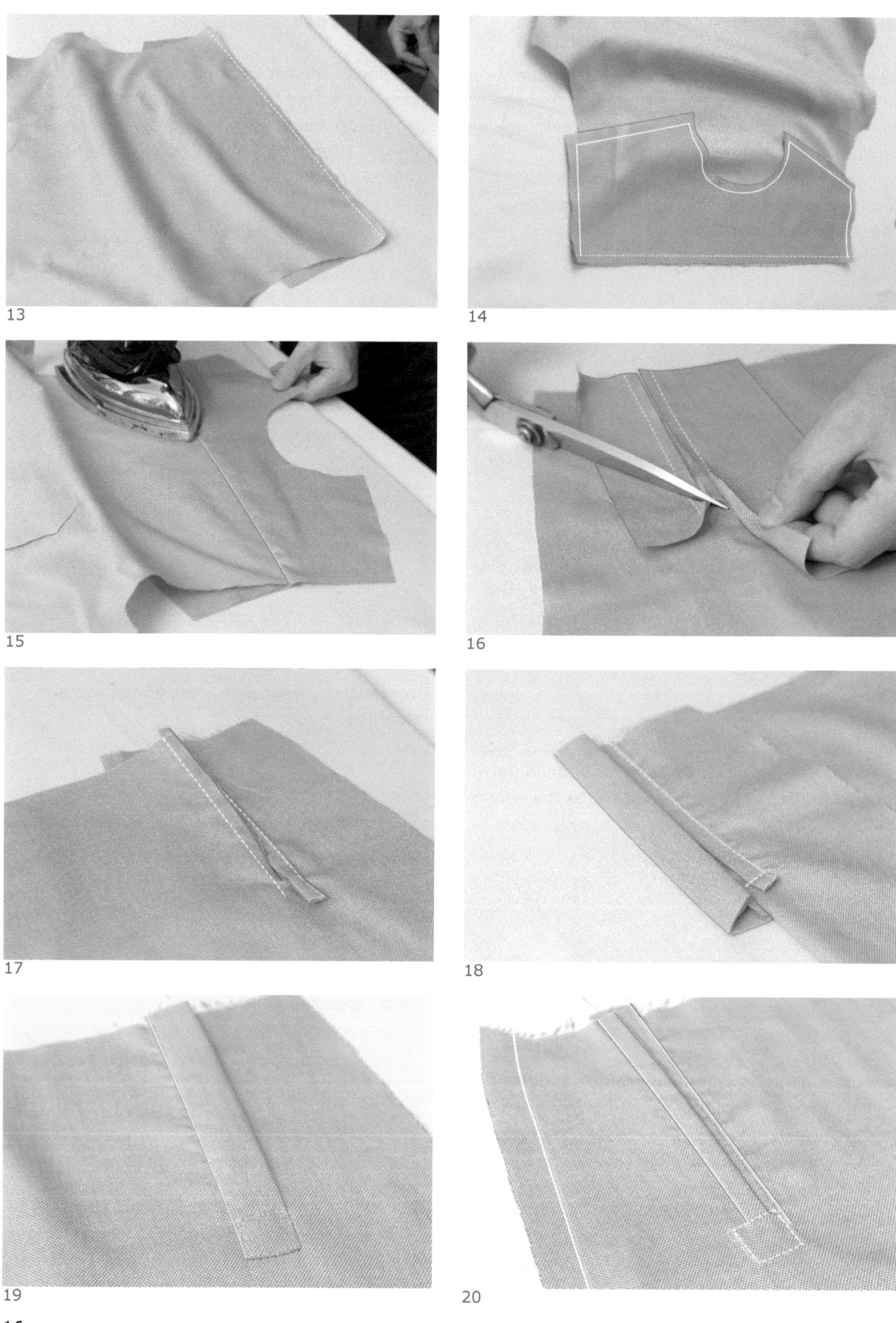

13

14

15

16

17

18

19

20

The back yoke

Picture 13

First, the inner back yoke is placed on the back. Facing the right fabric side of the yoke onto the left side of the back part and stitched with a narrow seam (0.5 cm).

Picture 14

The outer back yoke is then stitched with a regular wide seam (0.75 cm) on the back, facing the right fabric side of the yoke to the right side of the back.

Picture 15

Afterwards, both back yokes are ironed up one after the other. The back yoke can be fixed with a narrow seam (1 mm) if desired.

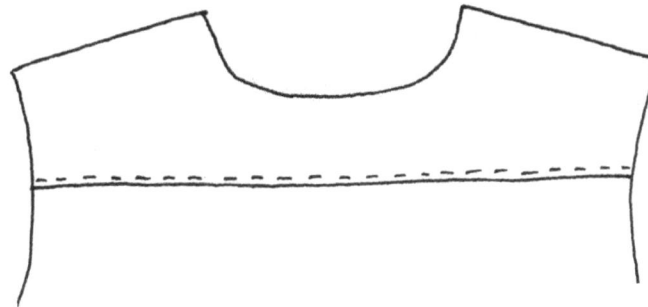

The sleeve vent

The binding and placket are stitched approximately 5 mm at the sleeve vent. The binding is on the narrow side, and the placket is on the wider side.

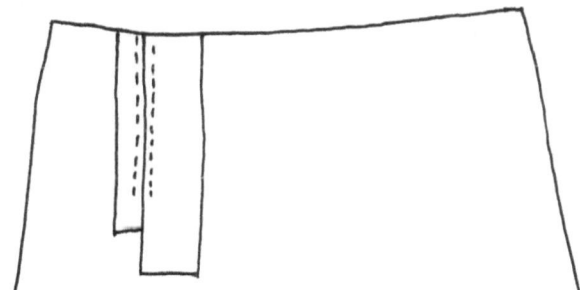

Picture 16

Now, the vent is cut open, and the corners at the end are pinched like a triangle until just before the last seam stitch.

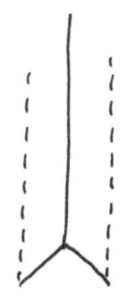

Picture 17

The binding is now folded and ironed twice by 0.5 cm and then stitched through at the top. If desired, the binding can also be hand-stitched with blind stitching and then machine-stitched from the top.

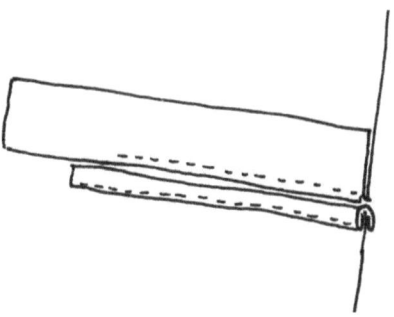

Now the binding is stitched together with the triangle; this way, the slit looks clean <u>inside</u>.

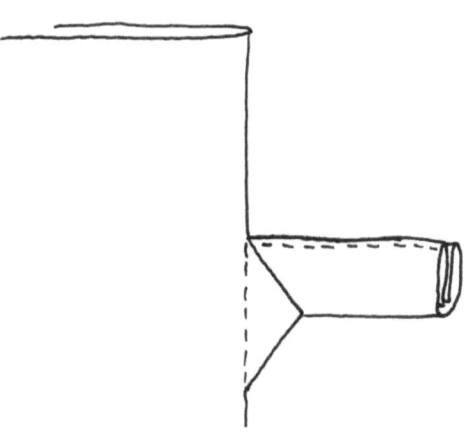

Picture 18

The placket is first folded and ironed by 1 cm and then by 2 cm. The end of the placket can be pointed or straight as you wish.

Picture 19

Then, the placket is stitched from the top. You have to be careful so that the placket is well caught. It is safer to hand-stitch the placket with a blind stitch and then machine stitch from the top.

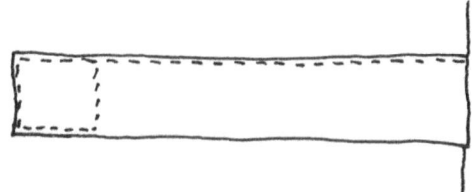

Picture 20

Now, the back of the sleeve vent looks clean and well-finished.

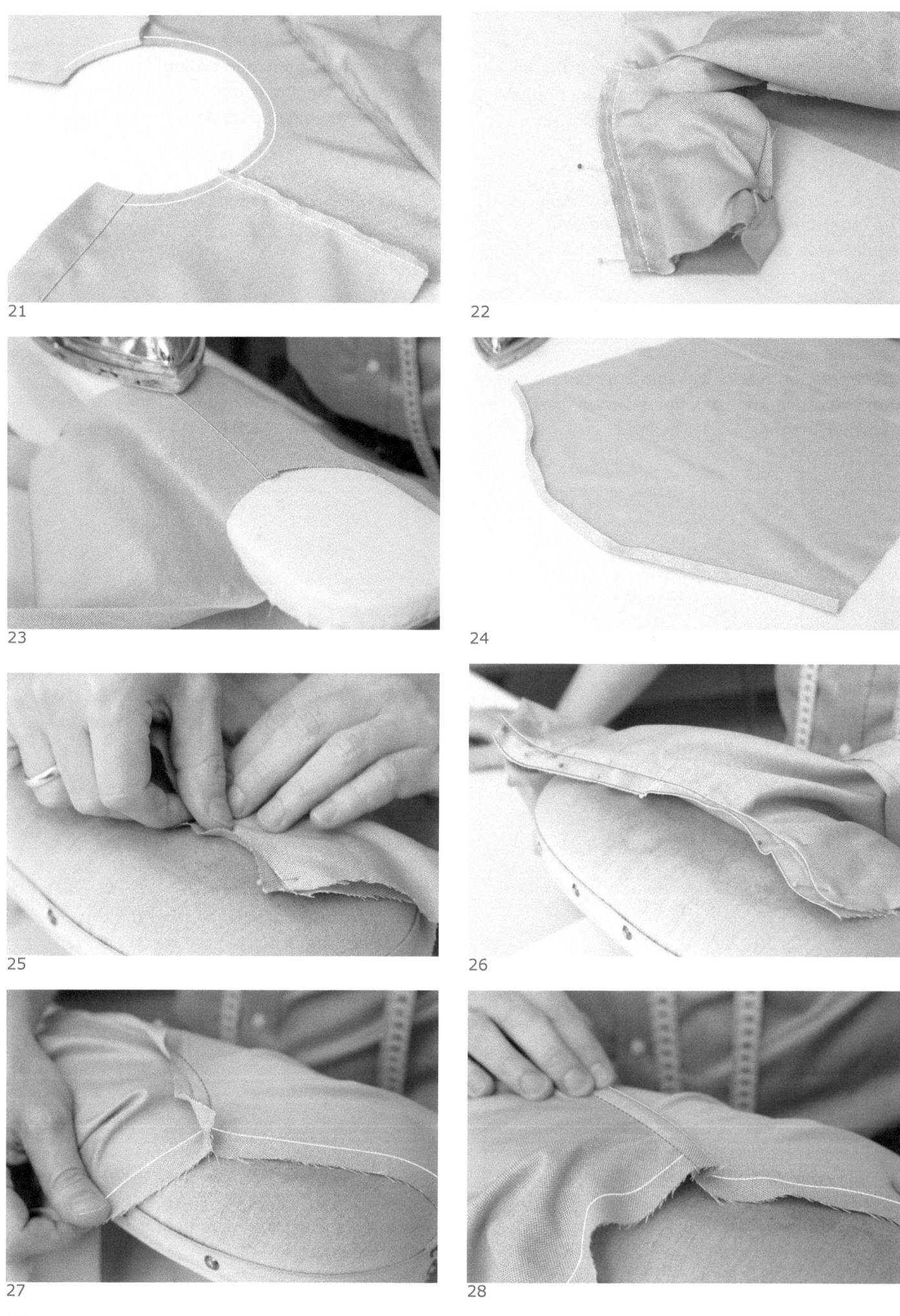

21

22

23

24

25

26

27

28

The shoulder seam

Picture 21

The shoulder of the front part is sewn to the back yoke with a narrow seam (5 mm) facing the right fabric sides together. (Attention, do not swap right and left shoulder)

Picture 22

Then, the front part with the left side of the fabric is put on the right side of the 2nd back yoke and stitched together with a regular seam (0.75 cm).
It's a bit unwieldy, but you get used to it. Alternatively, the shoulder seam of the inner back yoke can also be pressed over by the width of the seam allowance and blind stitched by hand to the shoulder seam.

Picture 23

After that, the shoulder seam is carefully ironed flat.

Attaching the sleeve

For a better fit, cut off approx. 1 cm at the front sleeve head (f=front). This also results in better freedom of movement, as the arms tend to be taken more forward.

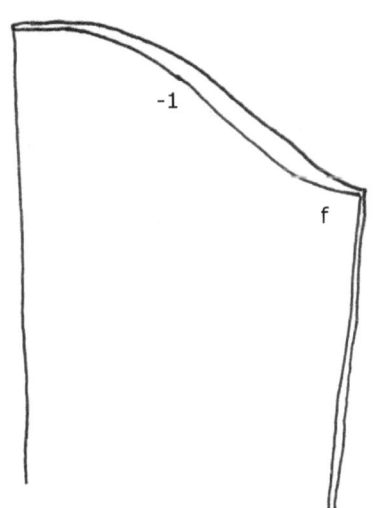

Picture 24

At the sleeve head, the cutting edge is folded down to the right side by approximately 0.75 cm. The picture shows the right side of the fabric. In the beginning, one often believes that it is wrong, but it will be explained in picture 28.

Pictures 25/26

Now, place the armhole's edge into the sleeve head's fold, facing the right fabric sides together. Ensure that the front part is pinned to the front section of the sleeve head.

Picture 27

Then, the sleeve is sewn onto the shirt. While sewing, the sleeve faces down to the sewing machine while the rest of the shirt lies on top. It is sewn on the front, back, and yoke, not the sleeve.

Picture 28

Finally, the seam is ironed flat so the previously folded sleeve head encloses the seam allowance of the armhole.

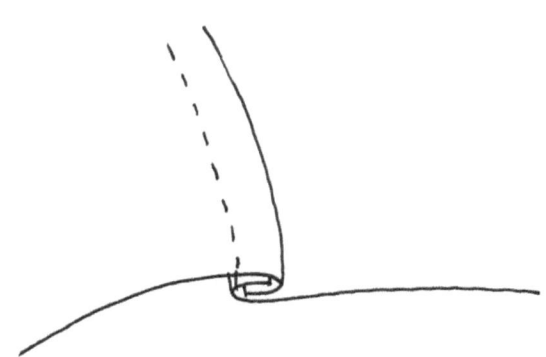

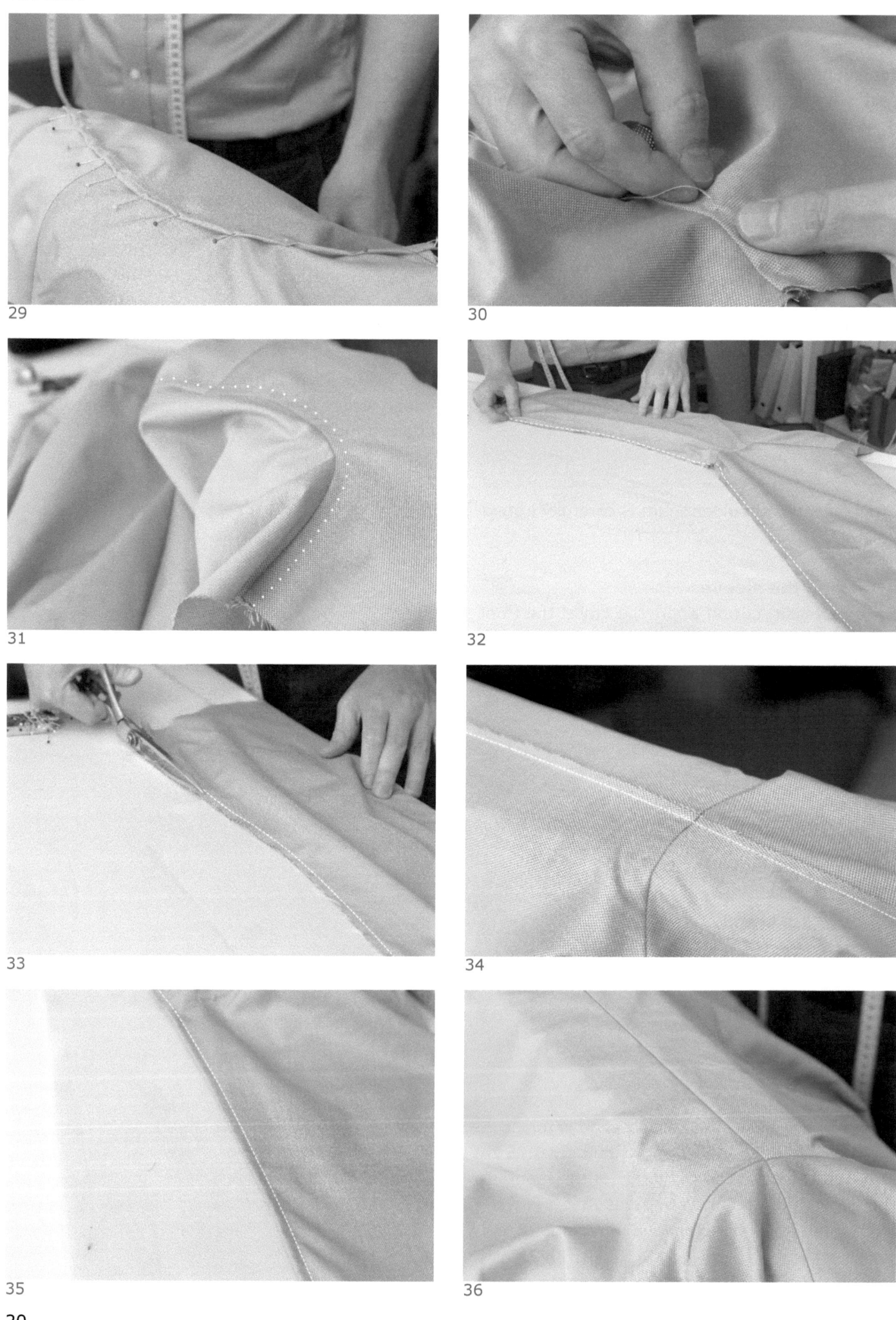

29

30

31

32

33

34

35

36

Wrapping the sleeve head seam

Picture 29

On the wrong side (the inside) of the fabric, the folded seam allowance is now fixed to the armhole with pins or a basting stitch.

Picture 30

Then, this folded seam can be fixed with a prick stitch (see page 11), which is approximately 0.75 cm wide. If you wish, the seam can also be stitched by machine.
With both methods, it is essential to ensure that the folded seam allowance is secured when sewing.

Picture 31

Finally, the seam is ironed flat again and should be smooth and without any tension.

Closing the side seam

Picture 32

The side seam is first assembled at the crossing point of the sleeve seam and the side seam, facing the wrong sides together. Then, the seam is pinned down to the hem and up at the sleeve. After that, the seam is stitched by approximately 0.75 mm.

Picture 33

Then, the seam allowance is cut back cleanly to approximately 5 mm.
No individual fringes should protrude. Otherwise, you will see this later on the outside of the side seam.

Picture 34

The seam allowance is now ironed flat in one direction on the sleeve board. The closed sleeve is then turned inside out.

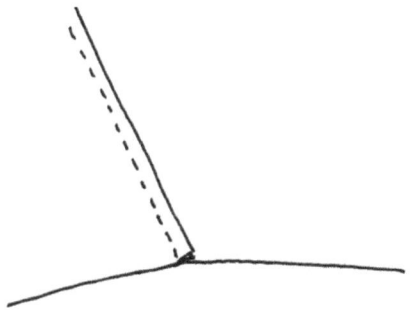

Picture 35

Now, the seam is ironed flat from the wrong side and stitched again with a regular seam (0.75 cm). This closes the side seam and makes it look clean inside.

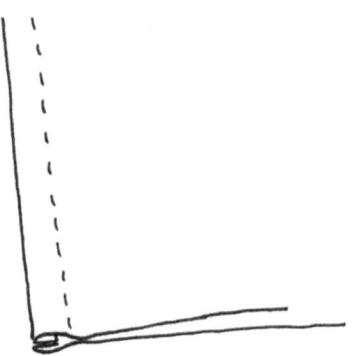

Picture 36

Finally, the sleeve is turned inside out, and the seam is folded and ironed flat to the back.
The seams at the armhole and the side seam should look like a cross and fit together perfectly. If care was taken when cutting back (picture 33), no fringes of the seam allowance should now protrude.

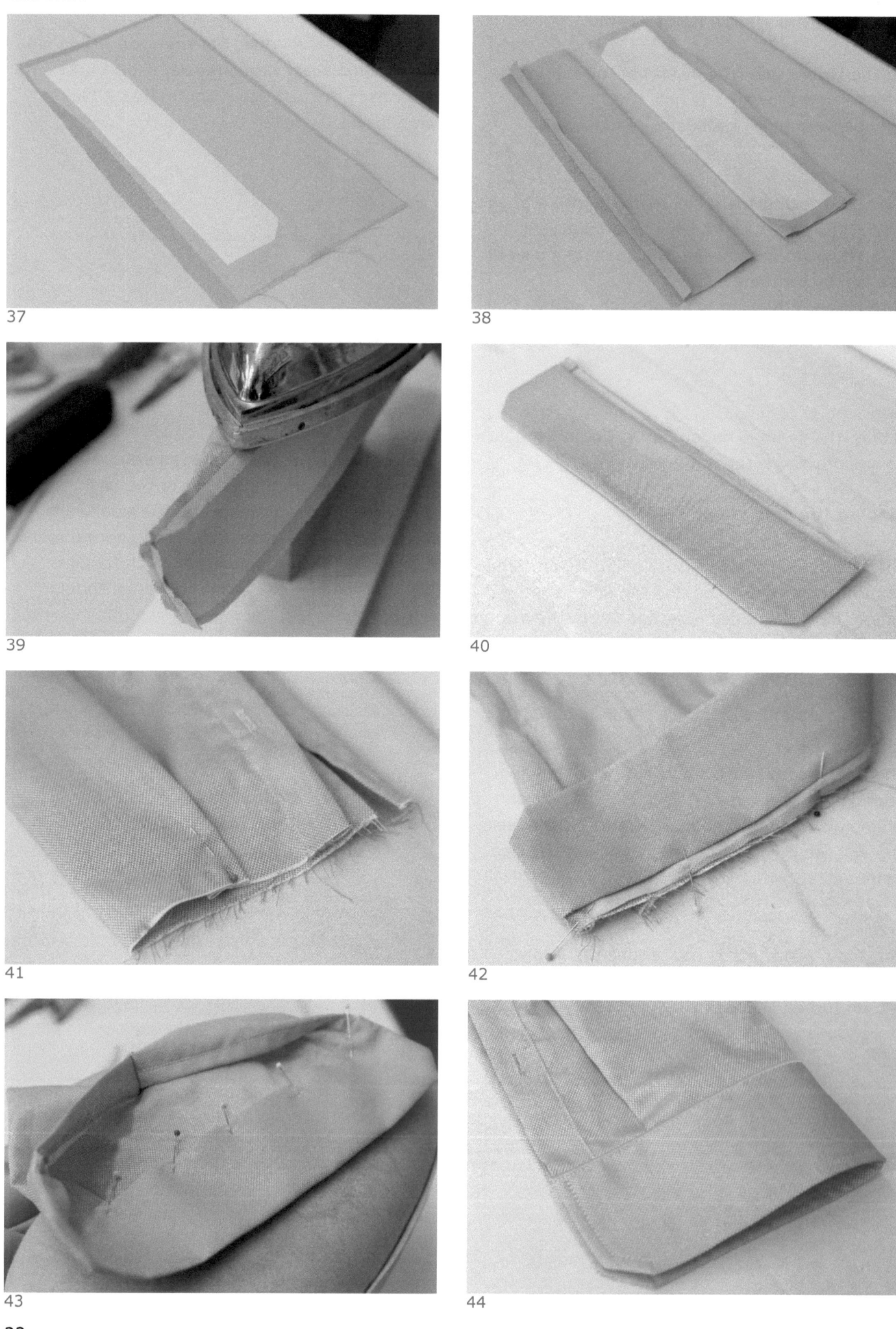

37

38

39

40

41

42

43

44

The cuffs

Picture 37

The entire cuff is first fused with a thin interlining to the wrong side of the fabric. Then, a thicker interlining is cut exactly in the shape of the cuff and fused to the previous fused interlining.

Picture 38

Now, the cuff is folded together, facing the right fabric sides together. At the lower side of the cuff, the seam allowance of 0.75 cm is folded up.
Then, the cuffs are stitched at the sides by 1 mm next to the thick interlining.

Picture 39

The seams are ironed flat, the seam allowances are graded down, and the corners are cut back.

Picture 40

Then, the cuff is turned inside out and ironed flat.

Picture 41

The fullness of the sleeve hem is placed in a fold, which is open towards the sleeve slit. (Some patterns may have 2 or 3 pleats)

Picture 42

Now, the cuff is put to the sleeve, facing the right side of the cuff to the right side of the sleeve. It should be ensured that the binding and the placket of the sleeve vent fit precisely into both ends of the cuff.
Missing or too much width can be adjusted at the fold.

Picture 43

The cuff is then stitched with a 0.75 cm seam and ironed flat. Inside the sleeve, the lower cuff is fixed with pins and closed with a blind stitch.

Picture 44

Finally, the cuff is stitched all around: first, sew about 1 mm next to the approached seam to the sleeve, and second, as a decorative seam at the outside by approximately 0.5 cm along the edges.

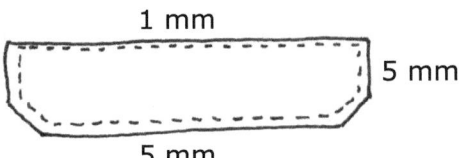

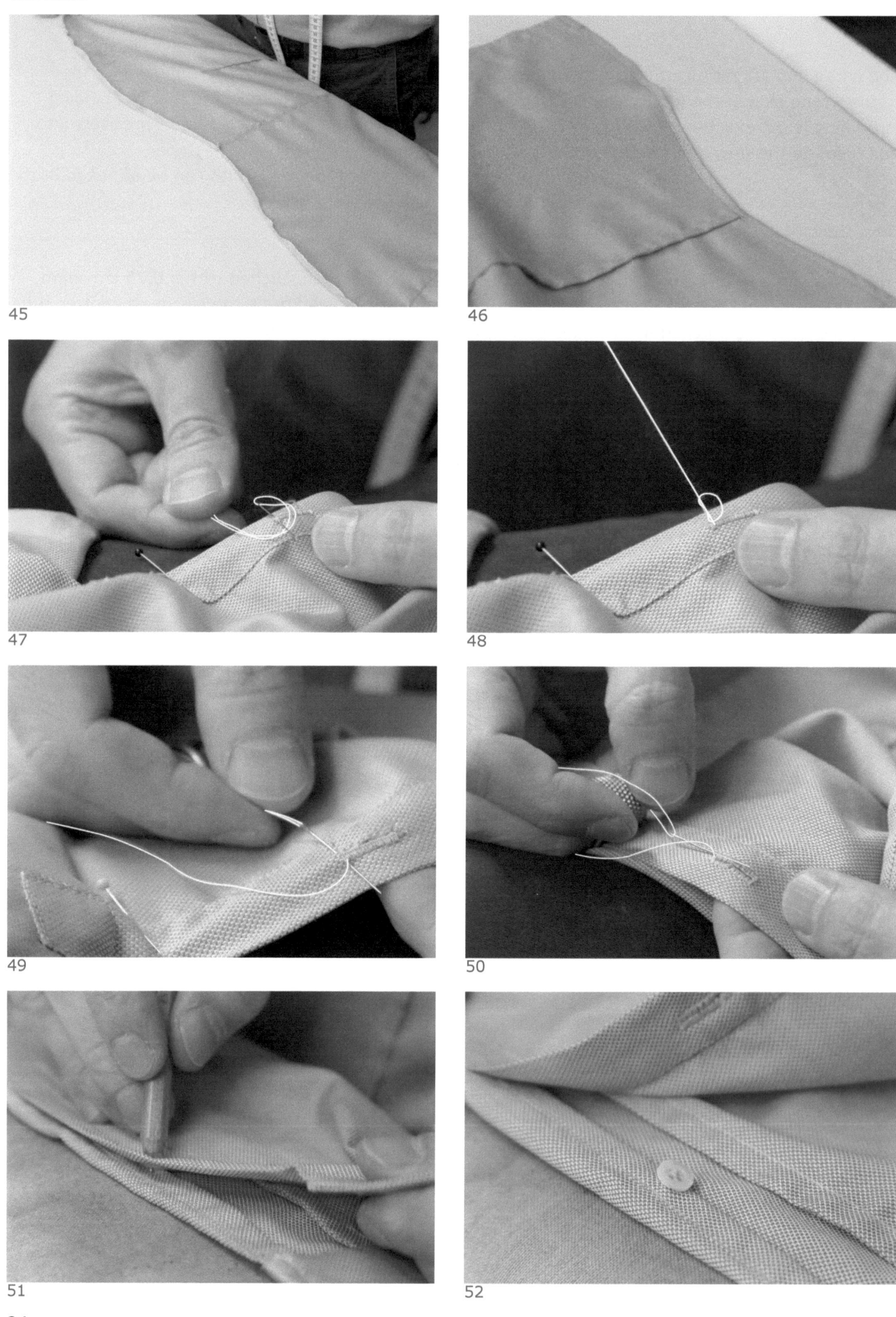

45

46

47

48

49

50

51

52

The hem

Picture 45

If the front and back hem lengths are different at the side seam, it has to be adjusted. Then, it is folded and ironed flat to the wrong side by approximately 0.5 cm. The narrower, the less inconspicuous and the more excellent it looks.

Picture 46

The hem is folded again and sewn evenly by hand or machine.

The buttonholes at the sleeve vent

Compare this with the buttonhole instruction on page 51. Shirt buttonholes are made with a thicker sewing thread (approx. 50 Tex). First, the buttonhole is machine stitched with a short stitch and cut open; then the gimp is placed.

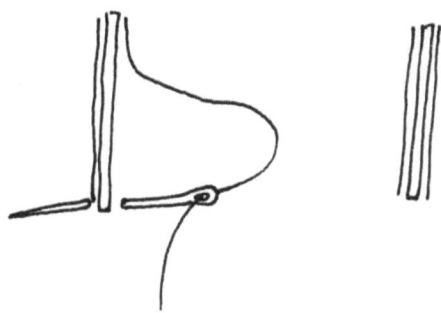

Lead the needle through the buttonhole and prick it out just below the stitching.

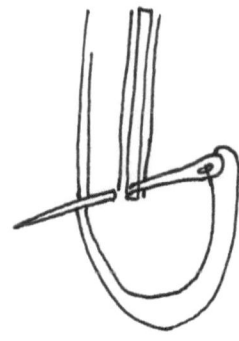

Picture 47

Place the thread under the needle from below.

Picture 48

Pick up the needle, pull up the thread, and close the forming nodule. The direction in which the thread is pulled is also the direction in which the nodule points.

Pierce close to the first knot at an even distance and repeat the process to the other end of the buttonhole.

Picture 49

Now, pierce up from below on the left end of the buttonhole. At the right end, pierce down again and create the bar.

After repeating the bar-stitch three times, pierce out in the middle of the buttonhole and tack down the bar again.

For the first stitch at the other side of the buttonhole, pierce up next to the bar, then pierce into the last knot from the previous side. Now pass the needle through the buttonhole and pierce out just behind the stitching.

Picture 50

Finish the buttonhole, create a bar at the other end and neaten up the thread at the back of the buttonhole.

Picture 51

Close the vent together to look pleasant, and mark the button position with a pencil in the centre of the buttonhole.

Picture 52

Sew on the button with a short stem precisely at the marking.

53

54

55

56

57

58

59

60

Fusing the collar

Picture 53

A thin interlining is pressed to one part of the collarstand and the collar turnover onto the wrong side of the fabric. Then, a thicker interlining, in the shape of the collarstand and the collar turnover, is pressed onto the thin interlining.

The collar stiffener tunnel

If desired, a tunnel for the collar stiffener is incorporated into the lower side of the collar. Here, the collar stiffener can be pushed inside. The collar is marked with the pattern, and then the position of the collar stiffener tunnel is drawn.

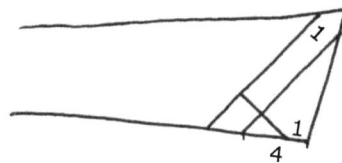

Picture 54

First, the undercollar is pinched at the tunnel mark.

Picture 55

Then, the corners at the cut are turned up to the wrong side to form triangles and stitched from the right side.

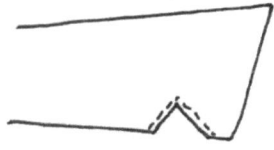

Picture 56

After that, the tunnel is marked with sublimation chalk on the right side of the fabric. Then, a piece of the shirt fabric is placed underneath (note the grainline).

Picture 57

Now, the underlaid fabric is stitched along the tunnel.

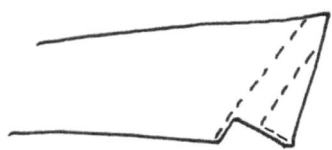

Picture 58

After stitching, the fabric is cut back slightly on the inside.

The collar turnover

Picture 59

Then, the collar turnover is placed together, facing the right fabric sides to each other. Now, it is machine-stitched by approximately 1 mm next to the thick interlining.

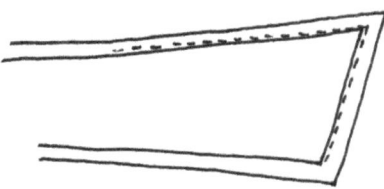

The seams are ironed flat, the seam allowances are graded down, and the corners are cut back.

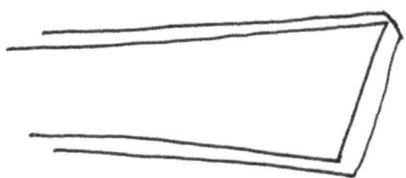

Then, the collar is turned inside out, ironed flat, and stitched by approximately 0.5 cm. When ironing, ensure that the collar-turnover's lower fabric is ironed slightly hidden. This means that the upper, visible part of the collar evenly covers the lower part.

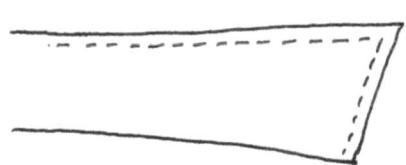

Picture 60

The part of the collar that is still open at the seam for the collar stand is now held slightly round and basted together. Thus, the lower part of the collar gets a bit short, and the form of the finished collar will be supported.

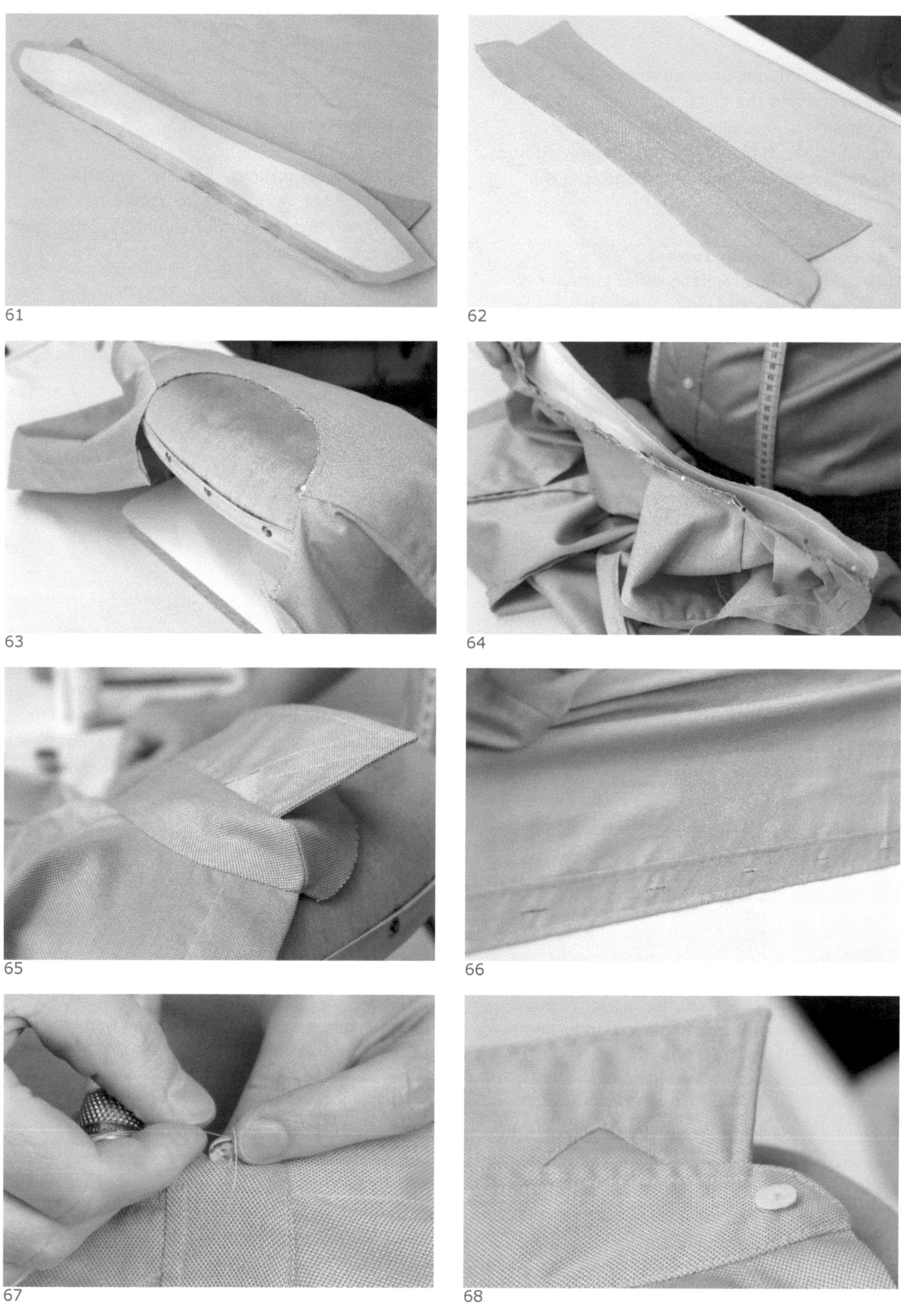

61

62

63

64

65

66

67

68

Attaching the collar stand

Picture 61

The collar stand is now placed in the middle of the collar. The fused part of the collar stand should lie on the stiff side of the collar and be stitched with a 5-mm seam. Then, the other part of the collar stand is pinned on and stitched by approximately 1 mm next to the thick interlining all around (except at the bottom of the collar-neck seam).

Picture 62

The seams are ironed flat, and the seam allowances are graded down. Then, the collar stand is turned inside out and ironed flat.

Attaching the collar

Picture 63

The shirt's neckline is placed neatly on an ironing pad, and the two parts of the back yoke are basted together. Then, the yoke is folded, and the mid-back is marked. Now, mark the mid-back of the collar.

Bild 64

The collar stand is pinned so that the unfused side faces outside and the fused side faces the neck.

Care should be taken to ensure that the front edges of the lower flap and the button bar fit precisely into the beginning and end of the collar stand.

Picture 65

Then, the collar stand is stitched seam-wide (0.75 cm). The seam is ironed flat and fixed with pins inside. If desired, the seam can be closed by hand with a blind stitch.
Finally, the collar stand is stitched all around - first by approximately 1 mm next to the neck seam and along the curve. At the approach seam to the collar turnover, the collar stand is stitched by approximately 5 mm.

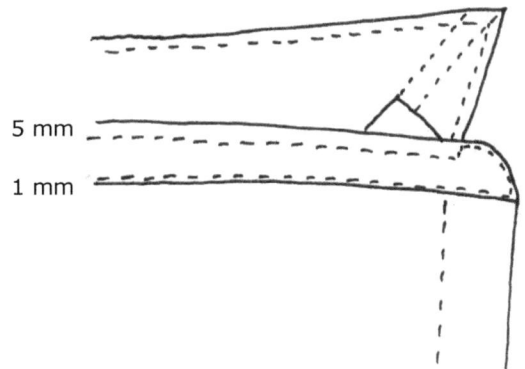

5 mm
1 mm

The buttonholes

Picture 66

The next step is making the buttonholes into the button placket and on the collar stand. These are now marked, stitched around, cut open and hand-sewn. See also page 24 (sleeve vent).The first buttonhole is approx. 6 cm below the neck seam. All other buttonholes have a distance of approx. 9 cm to each other.

Picture 67

After that, the positions of the buttons are marked. Place the button placket facing the right side onto the right side of the lower flap and mark the position with the pencil through the centre of the buttonholes.
Also, the collar is put together centred, and the button position is marked.
See also page 24, picture 51.

Picture 68

Finally, all buttons are sewn on with a short stem.

69

Link to the
trousers videos

https://www.becomeatailor.com/videos-trousers/

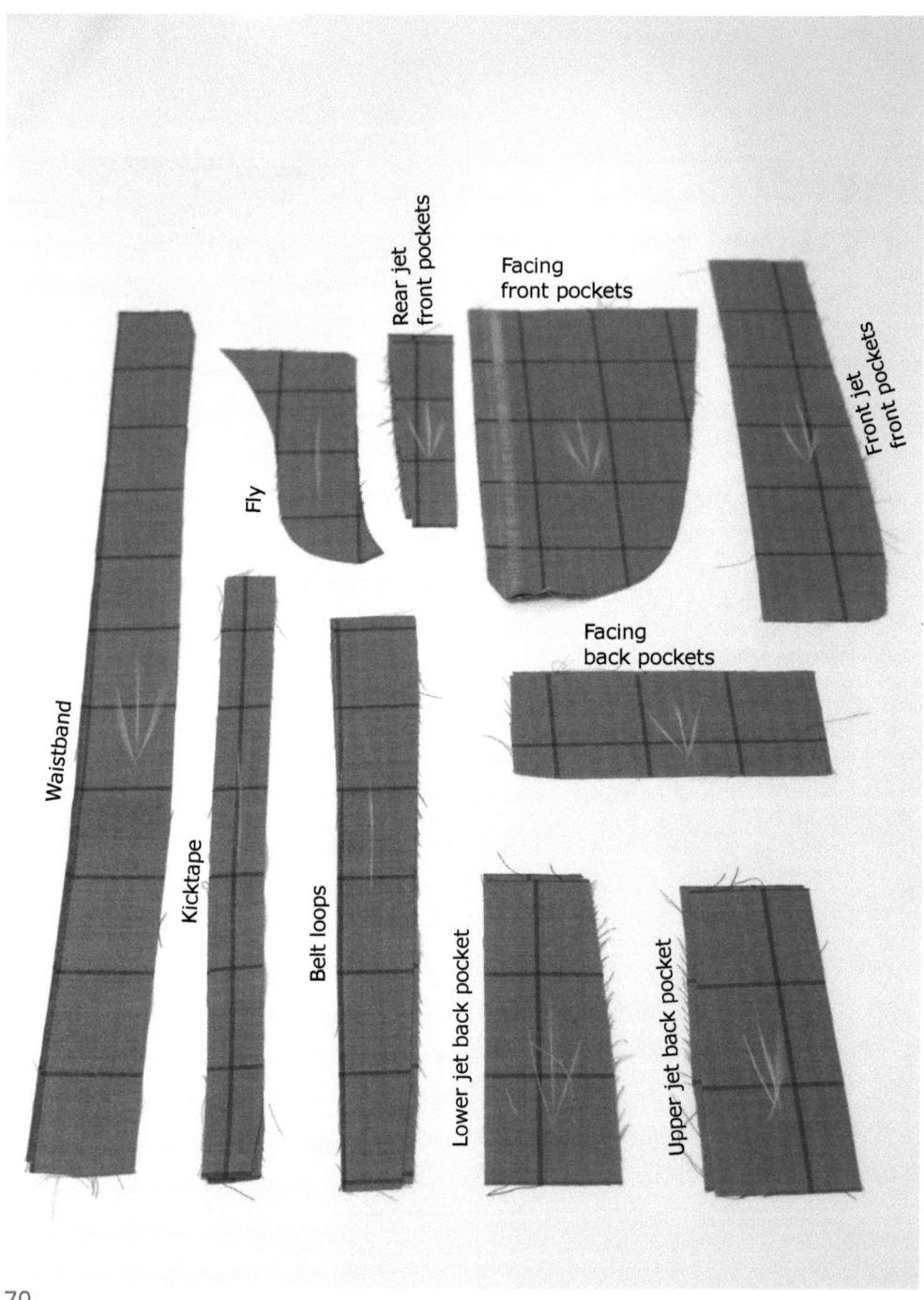

70

Measurements for accessories

Waistband: length 1/2 waist + 20 cm, width 5.5 cm

Kicktape: length *WOL* + 5 cm, width 3 cm

Belt loops: length 40 cm, width 3.5 cm

Back pockets, two jets: length 20 cm, width 5 cm

Back pockets, facing: width 20 cm, length 10 cm

Front pockets, rear jet: length 20 cm, width 5 cm

Front pockets, front jet: length 30 cm, width 5 cm

Fly, left and right: see templates on page 124.

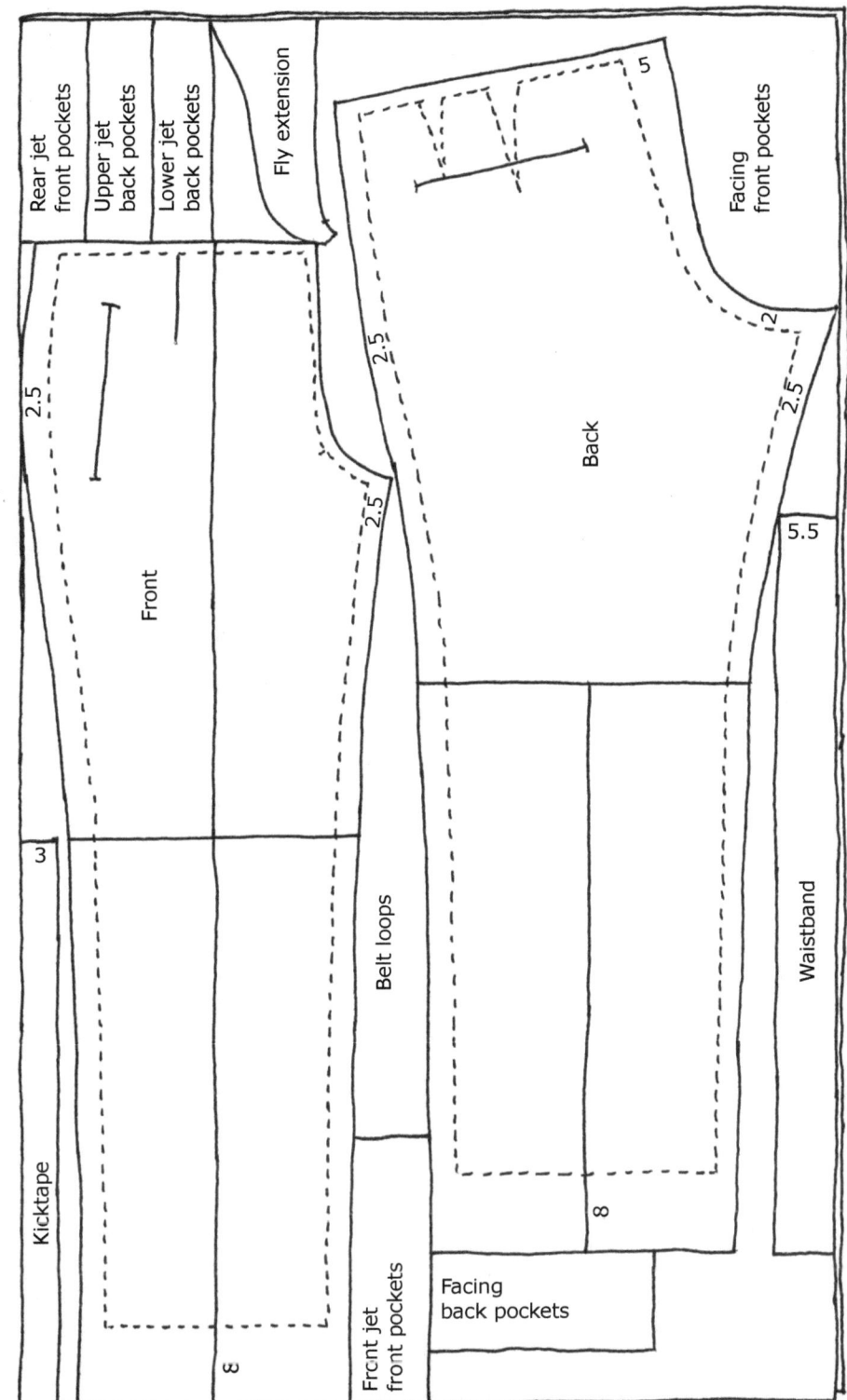

Cutting the trousers

For each fabric, paying attention to the grainline and the pile is essential. Breathe into your hand and stroke over the fabric. With a bit of practice, you feel the grainline and recognize the direction of the pile. Therefore, the back parts of the trousers are not cut against the pile to save fabric. Otherwise, it might shimmer slightly lighter or darker.

Please also note the explanation for the seam allowances on page 127.

Measurements for the pocketing

Pocketing for the back pockets:
Length 45 cm, width 20 cm
Waistband pocketing:
Length 1/2 waist + 10 cm, width 11.5 cm
Pocketing for the fly: Length 30 cm, width 15 cm
Pocketing for the front pockets:
see pictures 139/140 on page 52.
Waistband horsehair:
Length 1/2 waist + 15 cm, width 3.8 cm
(see page 63)

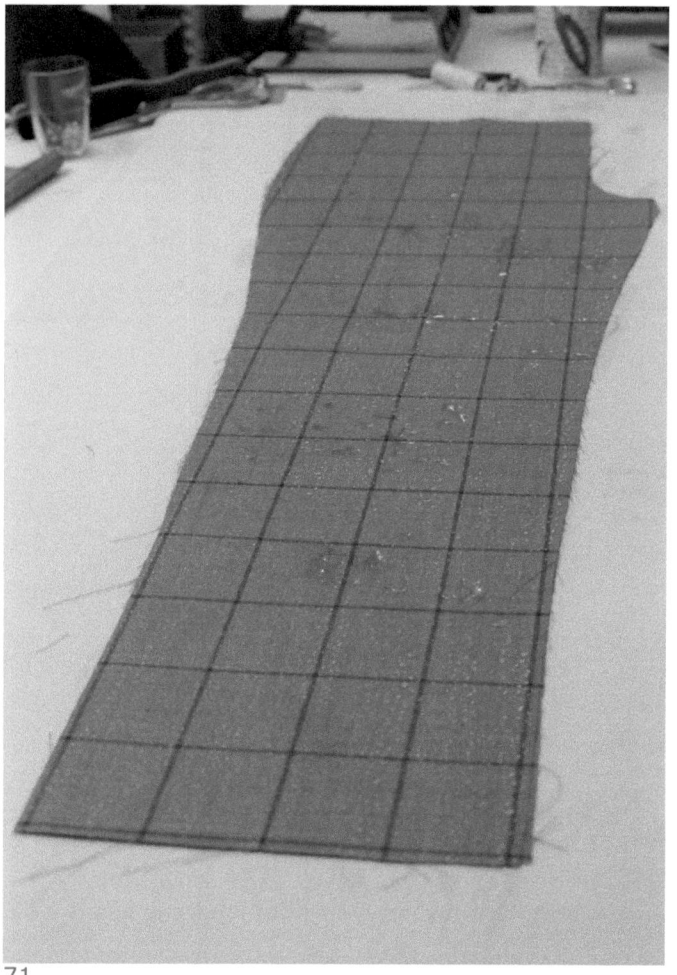

71

72

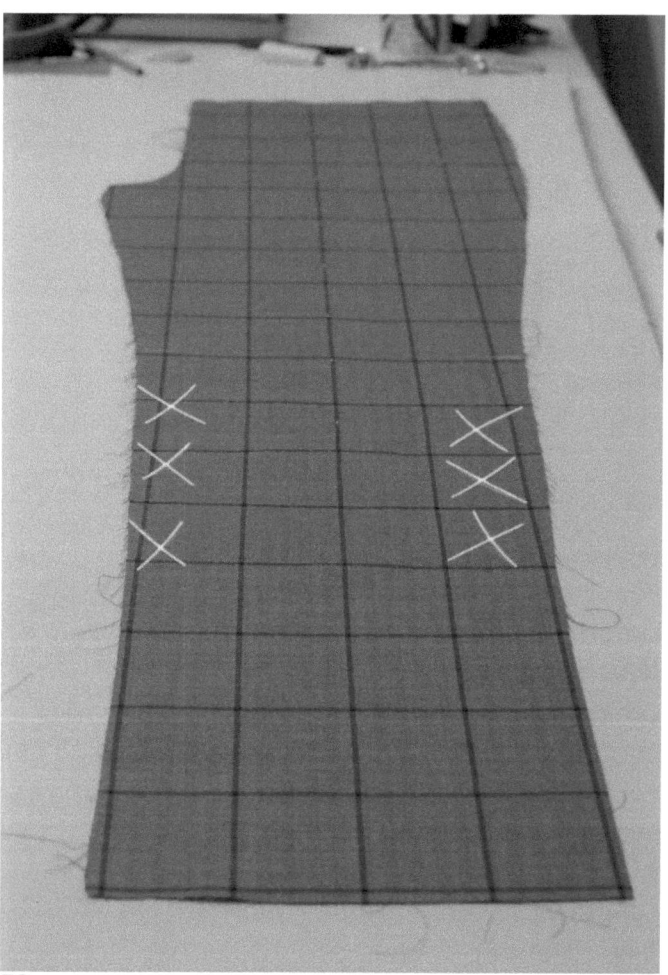

73

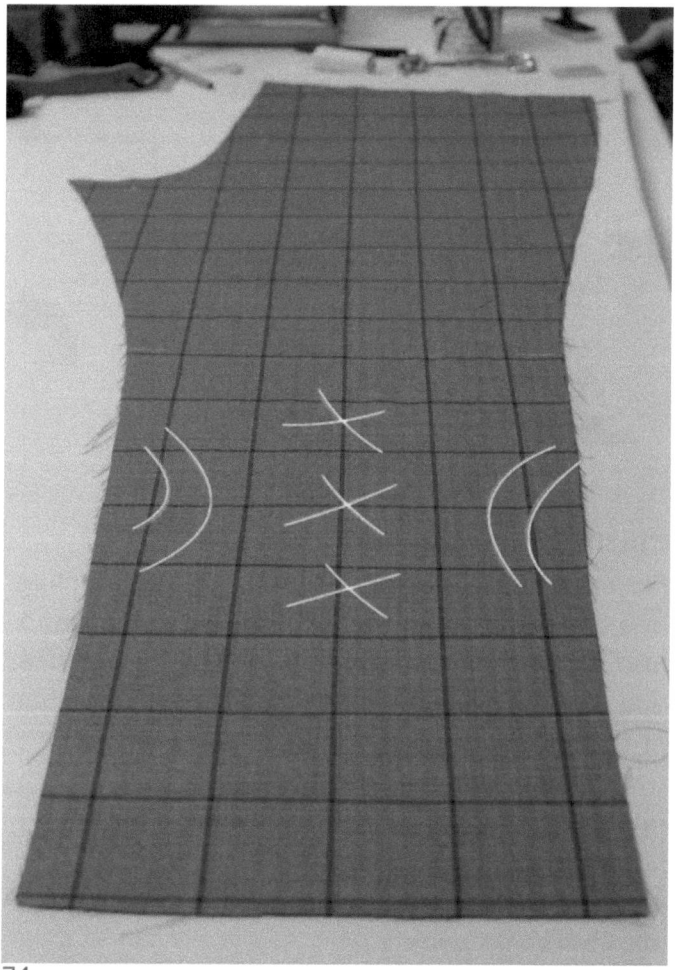

74

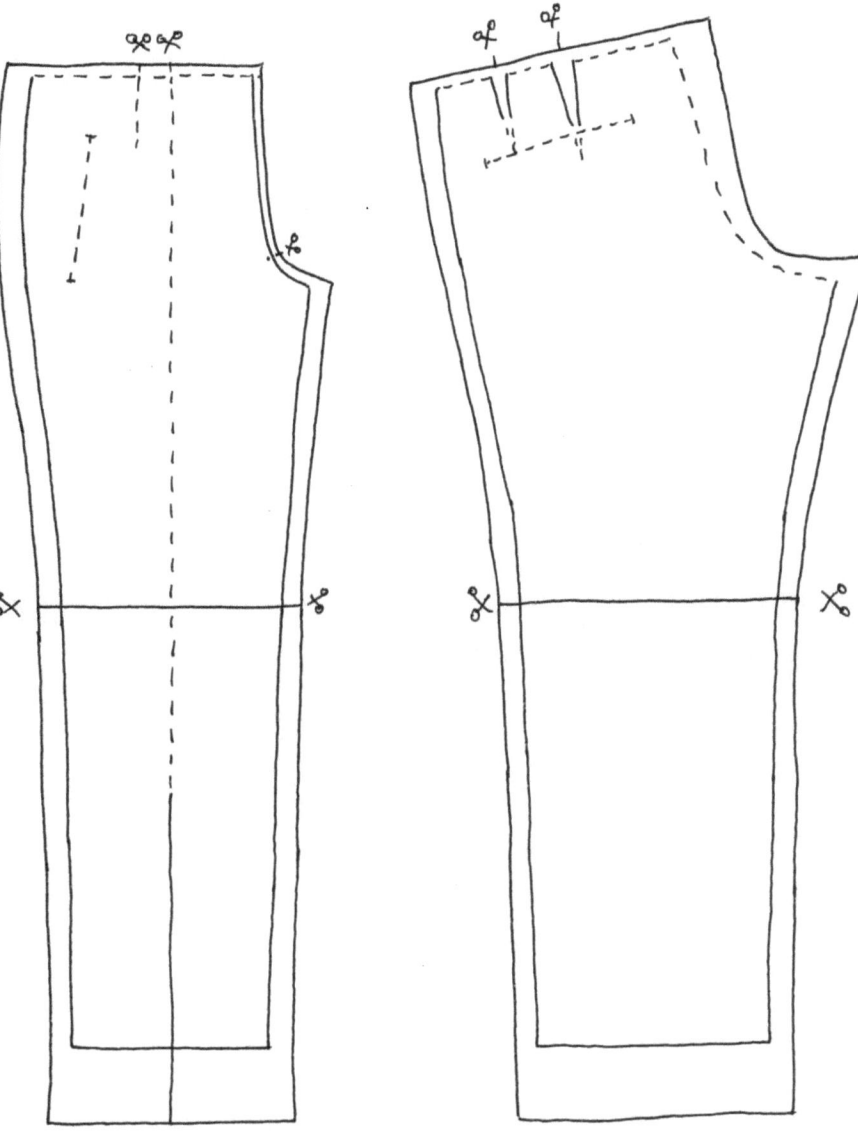

Tailor tacking

At the front trousers, tailor tacks are made at the following points: at the break-line (center front), at the pleat-line, at the pocket opening and at the waistline. At the end of the fly, the knee-point, the pleat-line and the crease-line, the marks are pinched in by approx. 4 mm.

At the back trousers, tailor tacks are made at the seat seam, at the darts' end, at the pocket opening, and at the waistline. The marks at th knee point and the beginning of the dart are pinched in by approximately 4 mm with the scissors.

On the left page, picture 71

The doubled cloth is made wet with a brush or a spray bottle.

Picture 72

Then, it can be carefully ironed dry. As a result, the cloth loses its tension, which it gained from weaving, and shrinks by about 1 - 2%.

The same is done from the other side so that both cloth parts are ironed.

Form pressing

Picture 73

The crosses stand for stretching; the curved lines mean keeping the area short.

The front pants are stretched below the knee point for the shape of the tibia. The same is done from the other side so that both cloth parts are ironed.

Picture 74

The back trousers are stretched below the knee point to fit the calf's shape and kept short at the outside and inside seams.

With a checkered fabric, the trousers can be form-pressed only after completion; otherwise, the fabric pattern does not match.

Above the knee-point, the inside seam is always stretched, contributing significantly to a better fit.

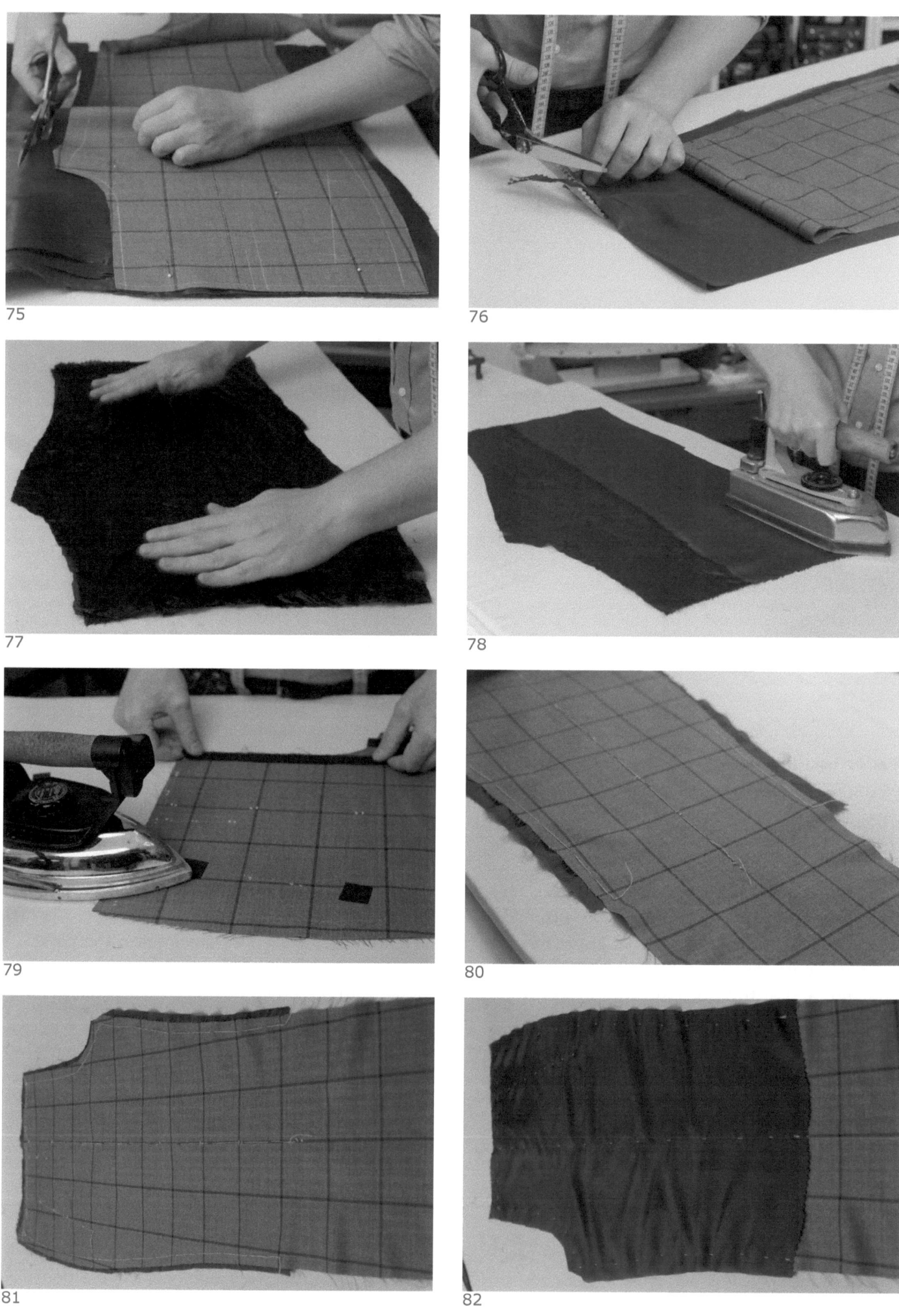

75

76

77

78

79

80

81

82

Dress to the left or right

What is meant by that? Extra width is necessary on the side where the "package" lays. This is the only way to create a perfectly fitting pair of trousers that is adapted to the men's natural conditions. Therefore, on the opposite side of the 'package', approximately 0.75 cm is cut away at the fly and crotch seams.

Simply place the other front-pants-part back about 0.75 cm from the center front and use it as a template. Both front parts should lie precisely on each other at the knee point again.

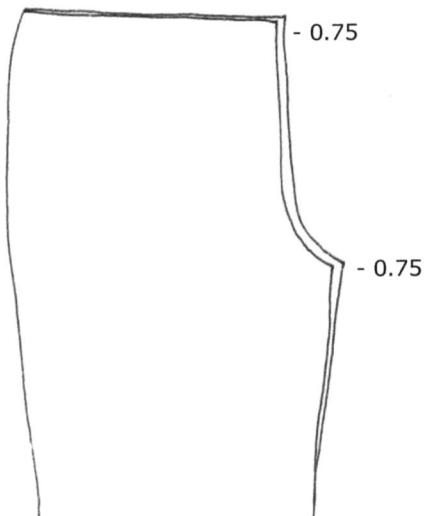

Cutting the front lining

Picture 75

When cutting the front lining, it should protrude at least 1.5 cm on the sides. For saving material, the grainline can run straight or across, depending on the length of the front trousers.

Picture 76

The lower end of the front lining is cut off evenly with the pinking shears. This prevents it from fraying. If the length is trimmed with the overlock sewing machine, the seam can be pressed through to the outer fabric.

Ironing the front lining

Picture 77

Then, the front lining is dipped in lukewarm water and then briefly wrung out. It can also be dampened using a spray bottle.

Picture 78

Now, the front lining can be ironed dry one by one with a heavy iron. However, with heat and humidity, the lining will shrink, which will prevent us from doing so later.

Securing the pocket openings

Picture 79

First, the vents and the ends of the pocket opening are secured with a stripe of a thin fusible interlining.

Basting the front lining

Picture 80

Then, the front trousers are placed onto the front lining and loosely basted at the center front (breakline). The upper material is smoothed out very softly, thereby the lining gets a little fullness (approximately 1 - 1.5 cm). The same is done at the side seam, the fly and the crotch seam. It is always basted from the waistband down.

Picture 81

Now, the lining is basted at the waistband seam and the pocket opening.

Picture 82

On the back, check to see if the lining's fullness is even. If it tenses or pulls in one place, the basting of the front lining should be redone.

Serging the front and back trousers

If all looks well, the outside seam, the fly, and the inside seam of the front trousers can be trimmed with the overlock sewing machine. At the back trousers, only the side seam and the inside seam are overlocked. The front lining is cut off with the knife of the overlock machine, and the edge is serged.

Alternatively, you can secure the edges with a zig-zag stitch or by hand.

If you use a zig-zag stitch to secure the edges and the lining, the lining will be cut back beforehand.

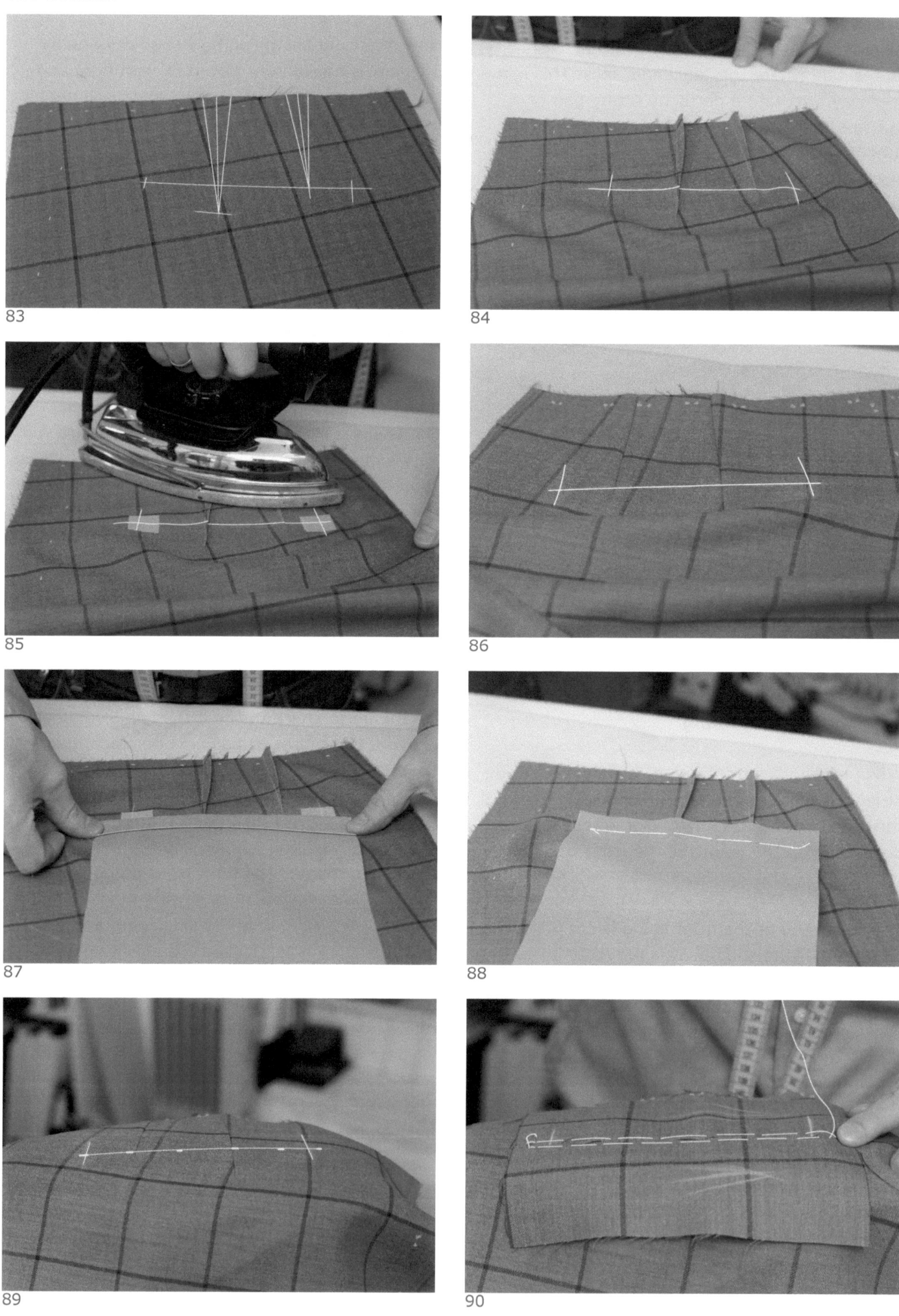

83

84

85

86

87

88

89

90

Closing the darts

Picture 83

The dart is redrawn and pressed at the center line. When sewing this seam, pay attention to the following: sew with a short stitch over the end of the dart and then knot the upper and lower thread.

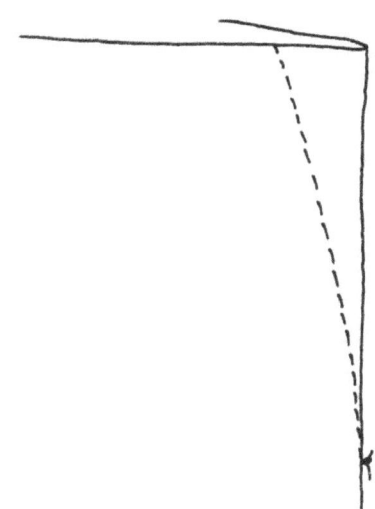

Or, sew over the end and stitch in again approx. 2 cm further up and lock (sew back and forth). Only now, cut off the thread. With both variants, an unsightly chunky end of the dart is avoided.

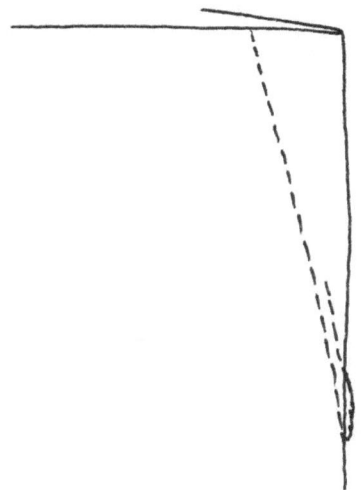

Picture 84

Now, the darts are pressed flat toward the side seam. The upper part of the back trousers at the waistband seam, which is no longer straight but round due to the darts is ironed in its form to support it.

Attaching the pocket bag

Picture 85

If necessary (with extremely fraying fabric or simply for safety), the ends of the pocket opening are secured with a very thin fusible interlining. It should be ensured that the pocket bag covers the interlining later.

Picture 86

The marking of the pocket opening is now transferred to the right side of the fabric.

Picture 87

Fold the pocket bag by approx. 2 cm to the wrong side of the fabric and place it onto the marking. At both ends, the pocket bag should protrude approx. 2 cm.

Picture 88

Fold back the folded part and attach it with a little width (a few millimetres) using a basting stitch.

Basting the jets

Pictures 89/90

Now, lay flat the back of the trousers on an ironing pad and attach the jets one after the other with a little length. At both jets, the grainline and the pile should run in the same direction (see the explanation for cutting on page 33). If there is a pattern in the fabric, it must match.

Then, the start and endpoints of the opening are transferred to the jets, and the jets are sewn on with a width of approximately 0.5 cm.

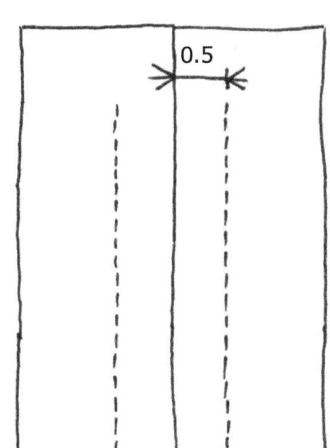

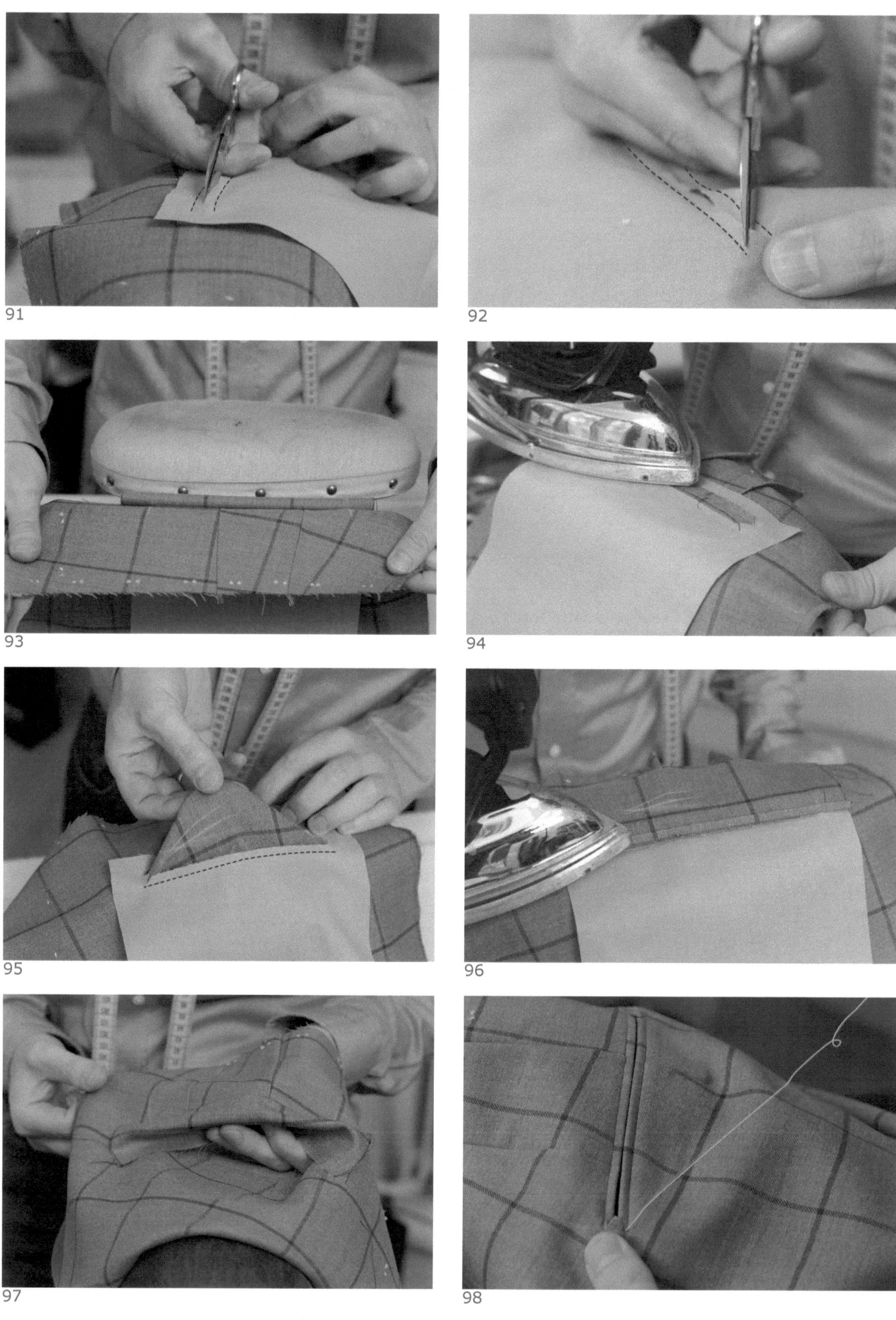

91

92

93

94

95

96

97

98

Cut open the pocket opening

Pictures 91/92

After checking the evenness of the seams and the ends, the pocket opening can be carefully cut open. Care must be taken to cut carefully and evenly so that later, the jets can be shaped alike.

The incision at the ends is made in the shape of a triangle and should be as close to the seam as possible, just before the end of the last stitch. Please pay attention to the seam allowances of the jets; they are pushed aside and not pinched!

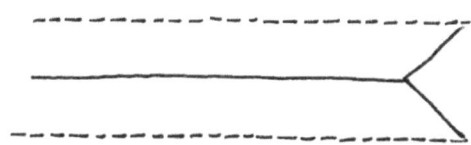

Press open the seam allowance of the jet

Picture 93

The back trousers are now held at the top of the waistband so that the upper jet hangs down. Now the back trousers can be pulled onto the pad carefully.

Picture 94

This means that the upper jet is folded over, and the seam allowance can be pressed open. The lower jet should lie completely flat. Pay particular attention to the work at the corners. This will make it easier to form and hand-sew the jets.

Pictures 95/96

Now, the lower jet is pulled through the pocket opening, and the seam allowance is carefully pressed open. Pulling out the lower jet can cause the upper jet to slip. Here too, make sure that everything lies flat on the inside.

Then, the upper jet is also pulled through the pocket opening.

Form and hand-sew the jet

Picture 97

After everything has been ironed flat adequately, the jets can be shaped.
The seam allowance of the jets will disappear into the folded jet.

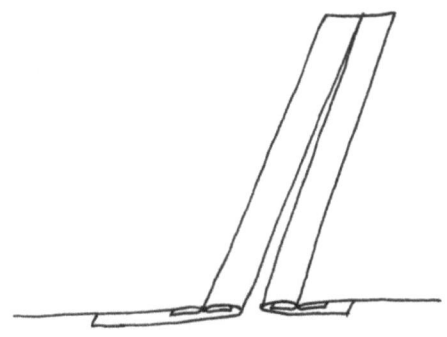

Then, the jet is sewn by hand with a point stitch exactly in the seam shadow. With the left hand the width of the jet is formed. It should be absolutely even by the width of approximatley 0.5 cm.
More, usually looks too chunky and less, too filigree.

Picture 98

In any case, it is important that the two jets together are as wide as the distance between the two jet-seams.

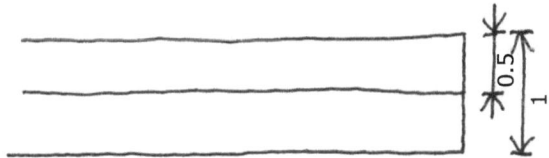

41

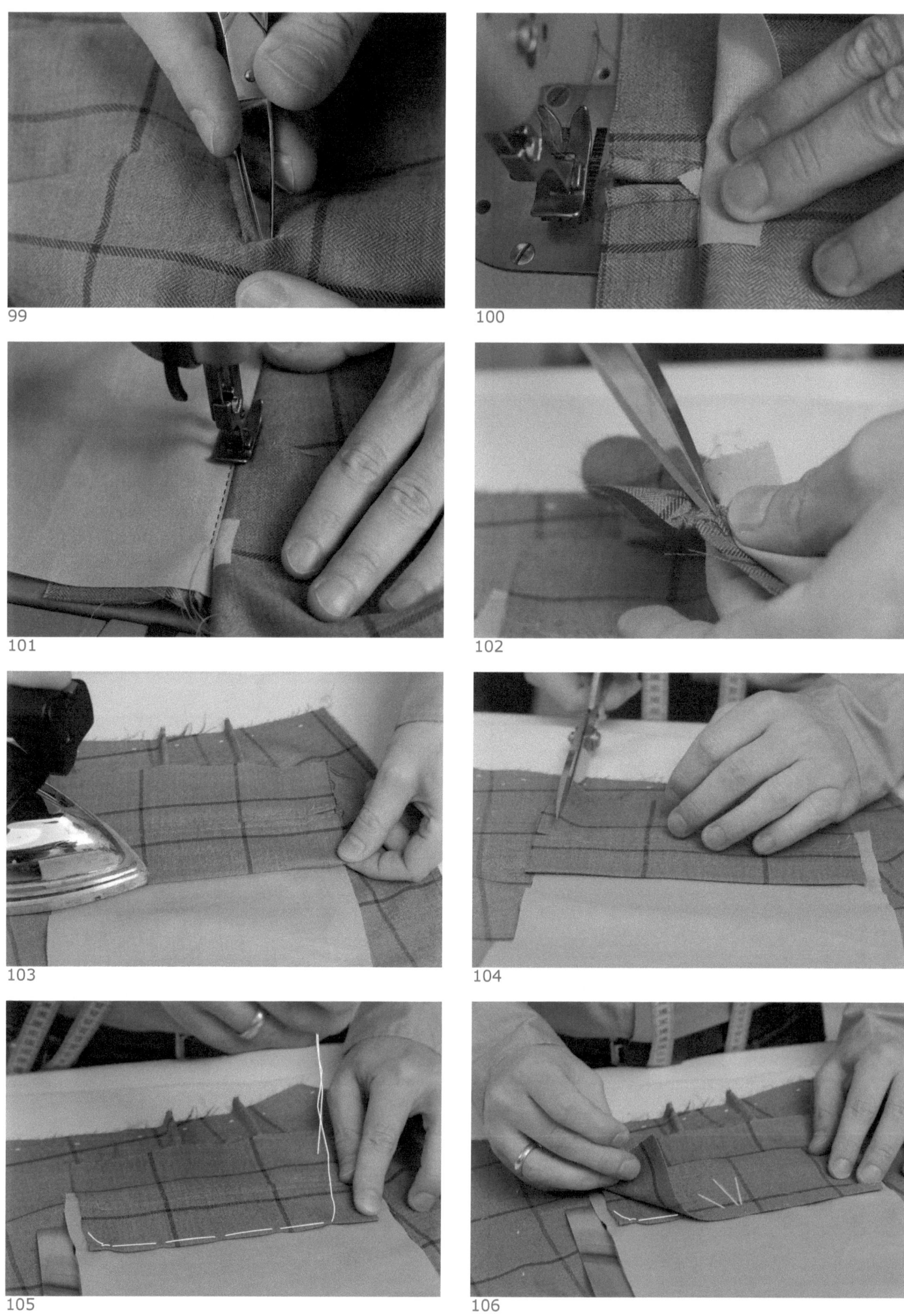

99

100

101

102

103

104

105

106

Basting together the pocket opening

Picture 99

The jets are basted together, and the triangled corners are carefully pushed inwards.

Securing the corners

Picture 100

Now, the corners can be secured with the sewing machine. Particular care should be taken here; otherwise, the corners might fray later. The sewing machine needle is inserted precisely in the corner. Then, it is sewn to the other corner, with the reverse back and forward again.

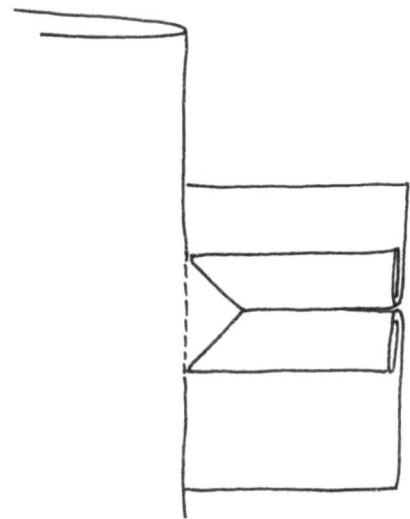

Picture 101

Then, the lower jet can be fixed from the back, making it more durable. For this, the pocket bag with the lower jet is placed to the right and the rest of the back trousers to the left.
(The picture is mirrored because we look at the sewing machine from behind).
Only the jet strip, previously sewn by hand, is stitched to the pocket bag. The outer fabric remains completely untouched.

Grading down the jets

Picture 102

Now, the jets are graded down at the ends. Two of the three layers are cut off. So the seam allowance can not bulge through to the front.

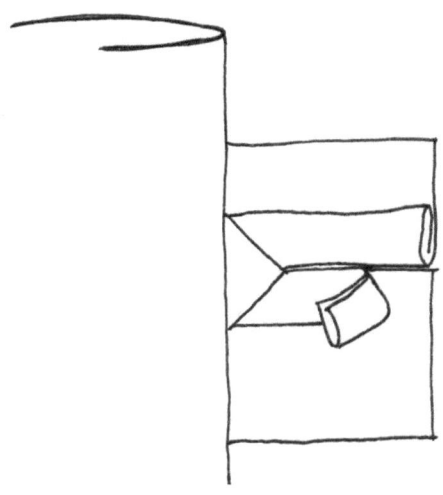

Picture 103

The lower edge of the jet is folded by 1 cm towards the wrong side and then ironed flat.

Trimming the jets

Picture 104

Both jets are cut off at the ends, making them approximately 0.75 cm narrower than the pocket bag.

Picture 105

After placing a piece of cardboard under the pocket bag, attach the lower jet without tacking the outer fabric.

Picture 106

The facing is also folded at the bottom to the wrong side and pressed flat. Then, it is placed, facing the right side down, onto the jet so that it is at least 1.5 cm above the seam of the upper jet. This means that the whole inside of the bag is graded and cannot bulge through to the front.

107

108

109

110

111

112

113

114

The pocket facing

Picture 107

Now, fold the pocket bag so that it protrudes about 1 cm above the waistband seam. Ensure that the depth of the pocket bag, measured from the opening, is approximately 17 cm. Use your fingers to press down the fold. Then, place one hand under the back of the trousers and the other hand on the pocket bag. Press the pants tightly between your hands and carefully flip them over to prevent the facing from slipping.

Picture 108

Carefully fold away the back trousers and attach the facing to the pocket bag. This is shortened at both ends to the same size as the jets, approx. 0.75 cm narrower than the pocket bag.
Then, secure the lower jet and stitch the facing to the pocket bag.

The buttonhole

Picture 109

The buttonhole should be marked in the middle of the pocket, and it should be located at a right angle approximately 0.5 cm below the jet seam. The buttonhole's size corresponds to the button's diameter plus approximately 2 mm.

Afterwards, it is secured all the way around with a small stitch.

Closing the pocket bag

Pictures 110/111

To close the pocket, take the two pieces of fabric and fold them together with the right sides facing each other. Then, sew up the sides of the pocket bag to secure the fabric in place.

Picture 112

Flip the pocket bag inside out and use an awl to smooth out the corners. Ensure that the jets, facing and seam allowance are lying flat.

Picture 113

Topstitch the edges of the pocket bag with a standard seam (0.75 cm), so that everything inside is also fixed.

Picture 114

Now fold back the upper part of the back trousers and close the pocket bag at the top. The upper part of the pocket bag, the upper jet, and the lower part of the pocket bag are connected.
Stitch on the pocket bag just next to the seam of the jet, making sure that nothing is shifted while sewing.
Sew through all layers except for the outer fabric. Thus, the upper jet is fixed and more durable.

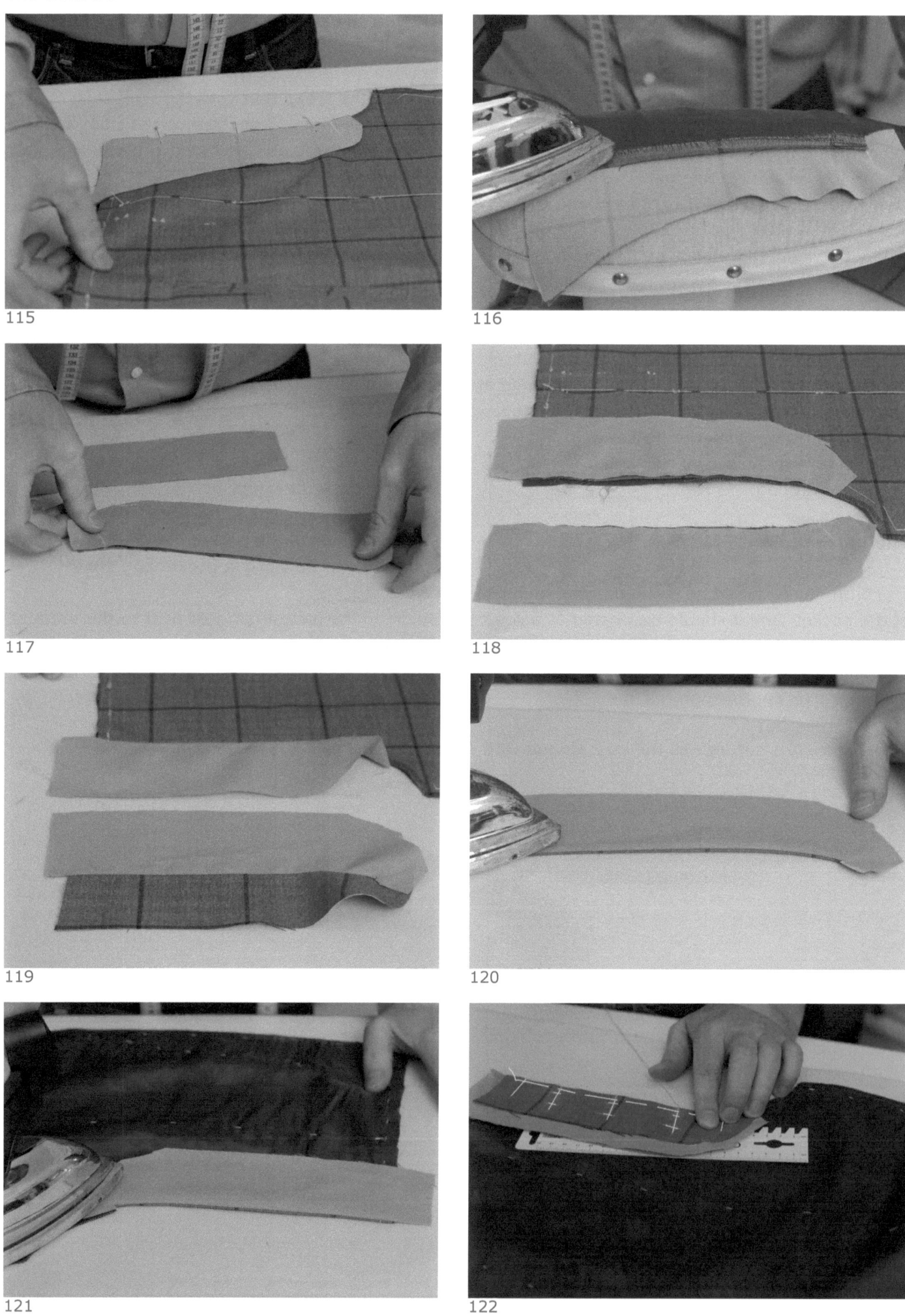

115

116

117

118

119

120

121

122

The right side of the fly

Picture 115

Pin the reinforced fly extension to the front trousers matching the fabric pattern, and mark the end of the seam.

Picture 116

After sewing, carefully pinch the seam allowance at the end of the seam. Then press open the seam allowances. The fly extension will be finished later (page 67, from picture 200).

The left side of the fly

Picture 117

Sew together the buttonhole placket and the facing (pocket lining). Then, and carefully pinch the seam allowance at the end of the seam.

Picture 118

At the fly, sew on the facing and carefully pinch the seam allowance at the end of the seam.

Picture 119

Iron flat the fly facing of the front and the buttonhole facing to one side and topstitch each by 1 mm.

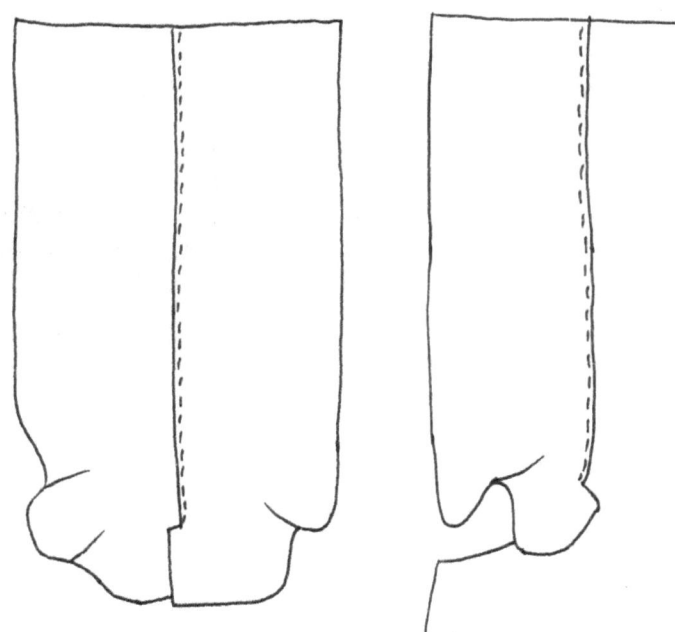

Picture 120

The buttonhole placket is turned over completely and pressed flat. Approx. 1 - 2 mm of the outer fabric should be visible.

Picture 121

The fly is turned over just like the buttonhole placket.

Marking the buttonholes

Mark the buttonholes on the placket and topstitch all around with a small stitch. The number of buttonholes depends on the length of the fly.
The distance between the buttonholes should be approximately 3.5 - 4.5 cm.
The size of a buttonhole should match the diameter of the button plus 2 mm.

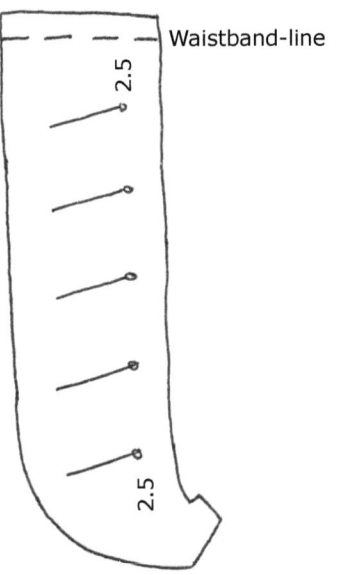

Waistband-line

2.5

2.5

Fixing the buttonhole placket

Picture 122

To attach the buttonhole placket to the fly of the front trousers, make sure it is placed approximately 1 mm back from the edge of the fly, and secure it with pins. Double-check the fabric pattern to ensure accuracy.

Next, place a gauge or a piece of cardboard under the unfinished end of the placket, and baste the three layers together using short stitches and a suitable thread.

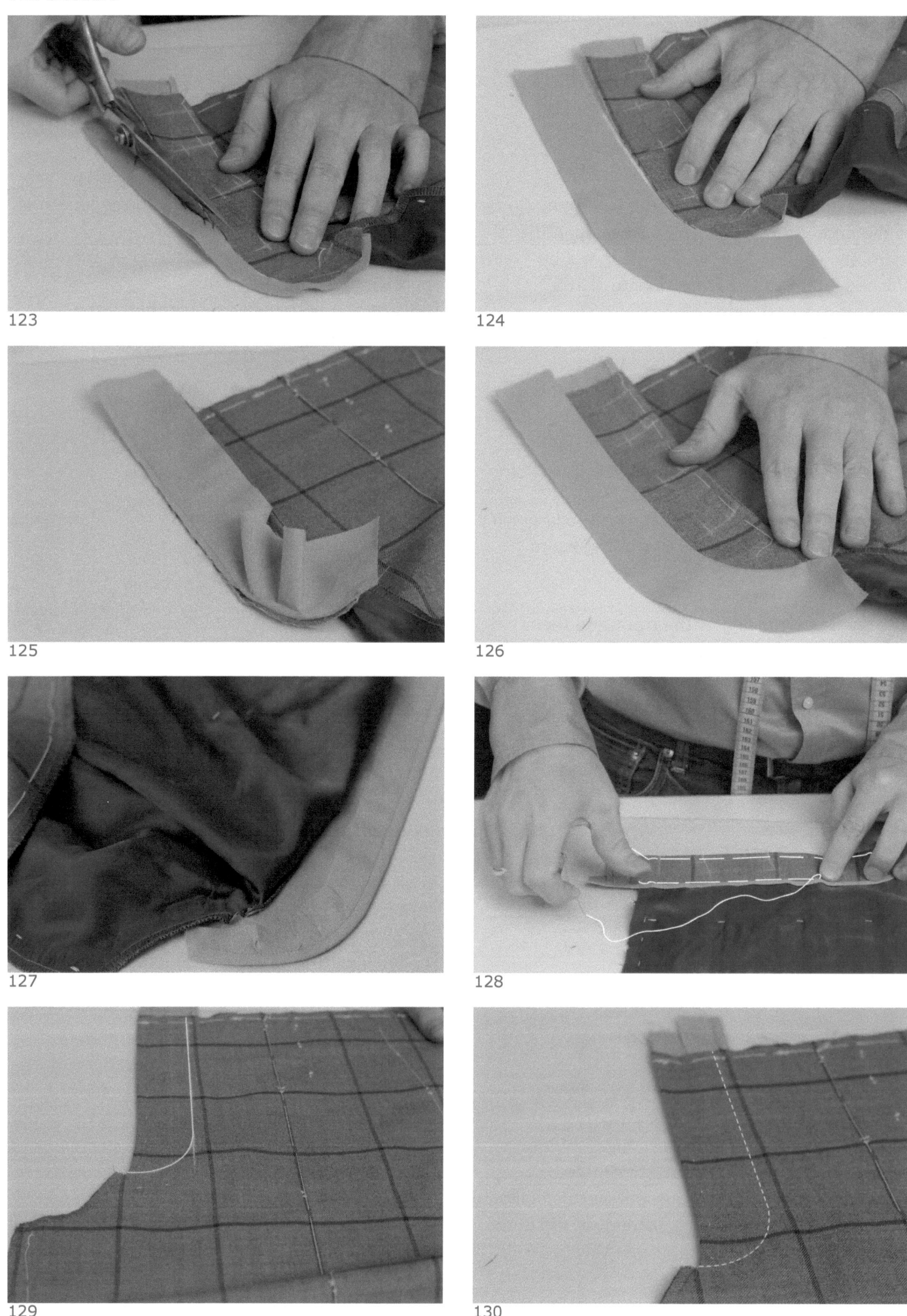

123

124

125

126

127

128

129

130

Binding the buttonhole placket

Picture 123

Now, the protruding lining is trimmed away evenly.

Picture 124

Cut a 3 cm wide strip from the pocket lining material in the shape of the buttonhole placket's edge.

Picture 125

Now, sew on the strip by approximately 0.5 cm.

Picture 126

Then iron over the lining strip and then fold it back so that only a 0.5 cm narrow binding is visible. Machine stitch evenly next to the binding.

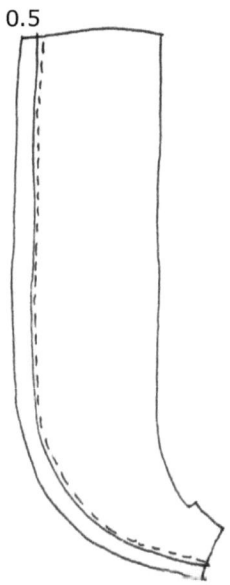

Picture 127

The fullness in the seam allowance of the binding is cut away, preventing any unsightly wrinkles from bulging through to the top.

Picture 128

The buttonhole placket is attached to the front trousers using basting stitches.

Topstitching the fly

Picture 129

On the top, mark approximately 3.5 - 4 cm for the seam, and draw a nice curve at the bottom. You can use a water glass or anything similar. (see page 112, picture 365).

Picture 130

To ensure a neat and secure seam, first lock the seam at the bottom briefly (3 mm) before stitching upwards along the marking. It is important to ensure that the outer fabric does not slip by the pressure of the sewing machine foot. To prevent this, you can place a ruler or a smooth piece of cardboard between the fabric and the sewing machine foot. This will prevent anything from slipping while sewing.

Once the stitching is complete, brush out any remaining chalk marks and give the fly a quick press with an iron to ensure it lays flat.

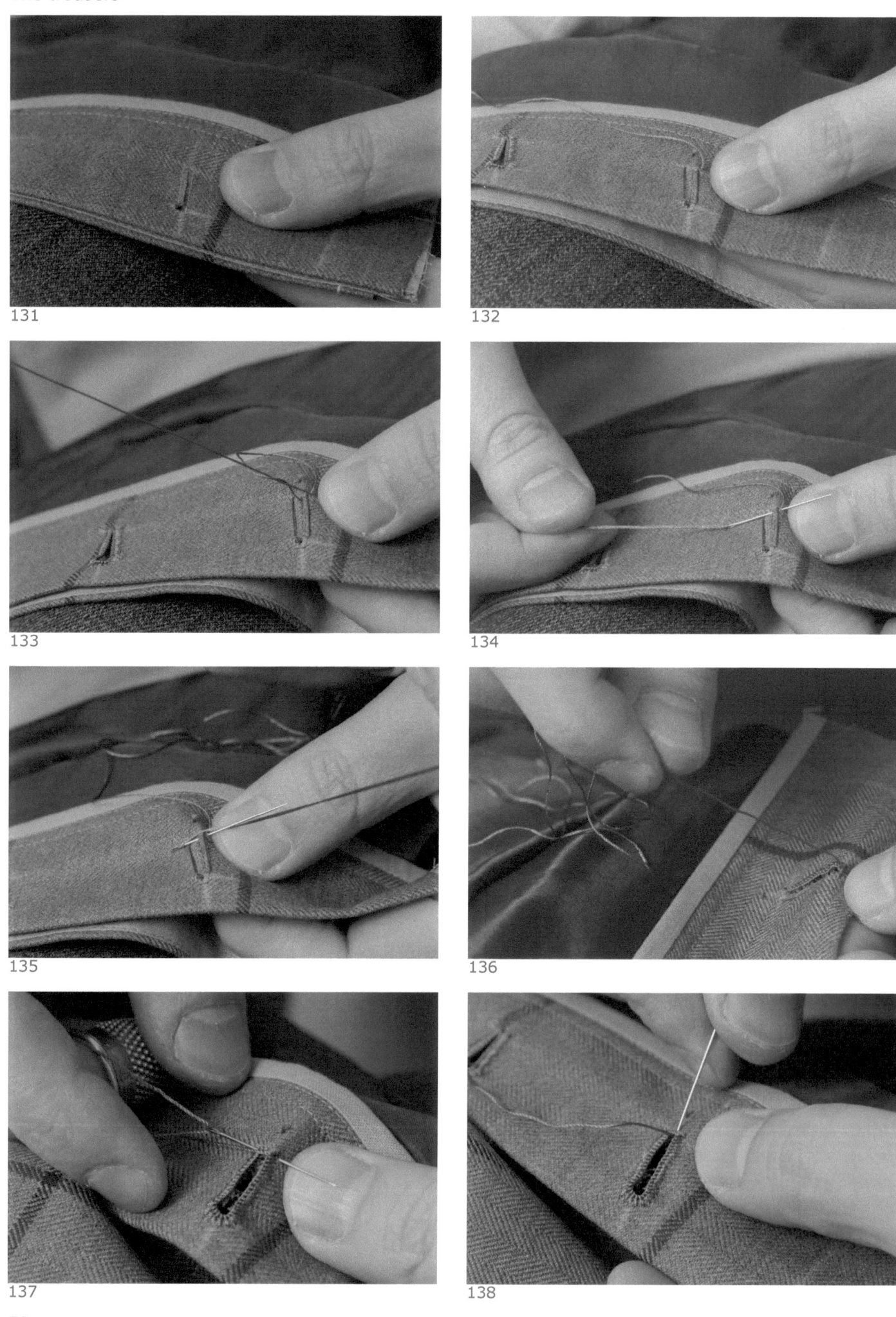

131

132

133

134

135

136

137

138

Buttonholes in the placket

Picture 131

The buttonholes are punched into the placket and cut open with care. For fraying fabrics, it is important to secure-stitch the buttonhole with a thin thread around the edges.

Picture 132

Then, the needle with the buttonhole thread is stitched around the buttonhole once to form a gimp.

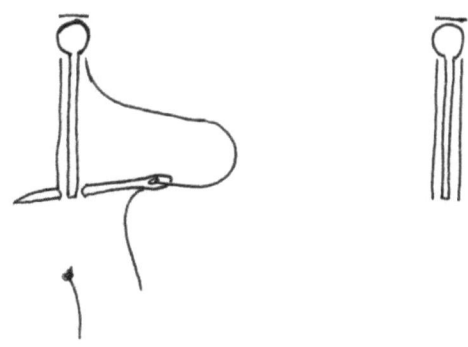

Picture 133

The needle is passed through the buttonhole and poked out from below, just behind the seam.

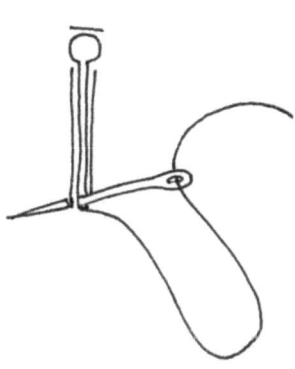

Pictures 134/135

Now, the thread is placed under the needle from below.

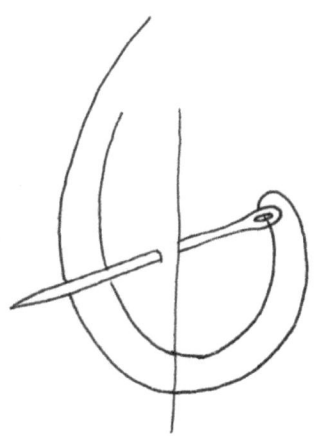

The needle is picked up again, the thread is pulled upward, and the nodule that forms is closed. The direction you pull will be the direction the nodule is pointing.

Now, pierce up behind the seam, right next to the first knot, at an even distance and repeat the process until you have sewn around the entire buttonhole.

Picture 136

Stitch the nodules narrower or broader to even them at the eyelet, like in the picture below.

After the last buttonhole stitch, pinch the needle through the first knot. Now, pierce down in the middle at the end of the buttonhole.

Picture 137

Then, poke upward at the left end of the buttonhole from below, pierce down again at the right end and make two bartacks.

Picture 138

After the second bartack, pierce upward in the middle of the buttonhole and back down over the bartack.

Finally, secure the end of the thread by sewing it into the buttonhole stitches on the back, then cut it off.

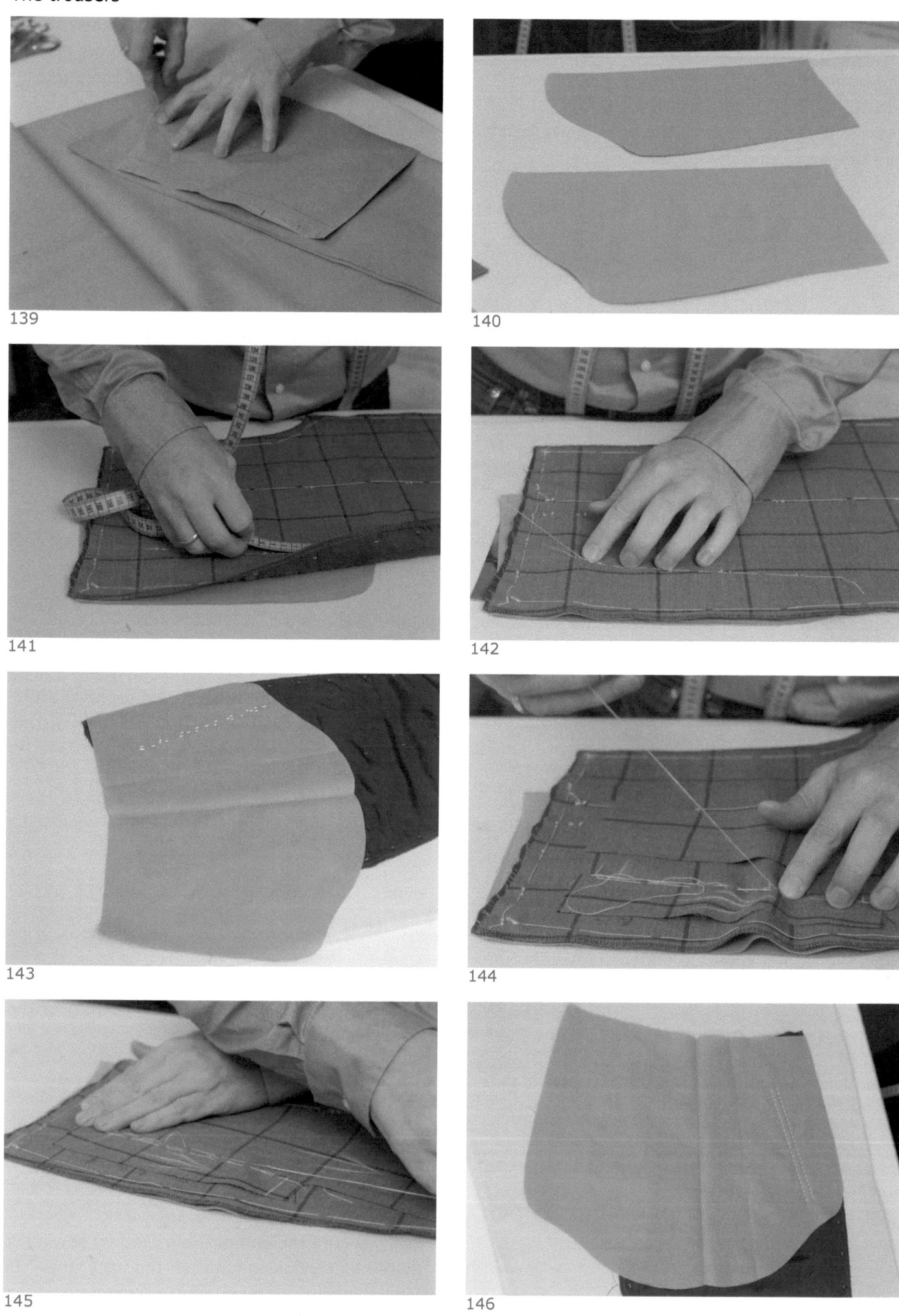

139

140

141

142

143

144

145

146

Cutting the pocket bag

Picture 139

Use the template from page 122 to draw the pocket bag onto the pocket lining with tailor chalk.

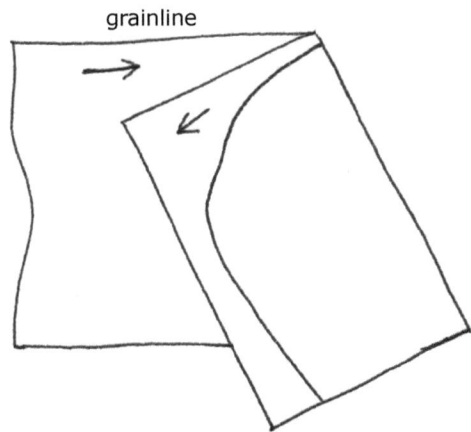

grainline

The pocket lining is turned over in the fold, causing one side of the pocket bag to be at an angle to the grainline.
This prevents the pocket bag from being too short in the pocket opening.

Picture 140

Iron flat both pocket bags.

Basting the pocket bag

Picture 141

Now, place the front trousers onto the pocket bag. At the top of the waistband seam, approx. 1 cm should protrude. At the side seam, the pocket bag should lie directly at the edge. The part of the pocket bag with the angled grainline must be facing toward the front trousers.

Picture 142

Then, a piece of cardboard is placed into the pocket bag so that only one layer is caught when basting. Now, baste through the marking at the pocket opening.

Picture 143

The pocket bag should lie flat.

Basting the jets

Pictures 144/145

Baste on both jets, one after the other, with a little length (a few millimetres). Here, the grainline and the pile should run in the same direction at both jets. If there is a pattern in the fabric, it must match.

Now, the start and endpoints of the pocket opening are marked. The jets are sewn by a seam of approximately 0.5 cm each. The seam is carefully secured at the beginning and end (sewing back and forth).

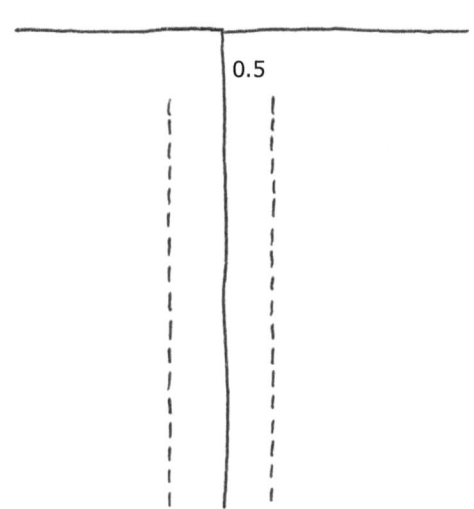

0.5

Picture 146

Then, check if the seams are straight and even and remove the basting threads.

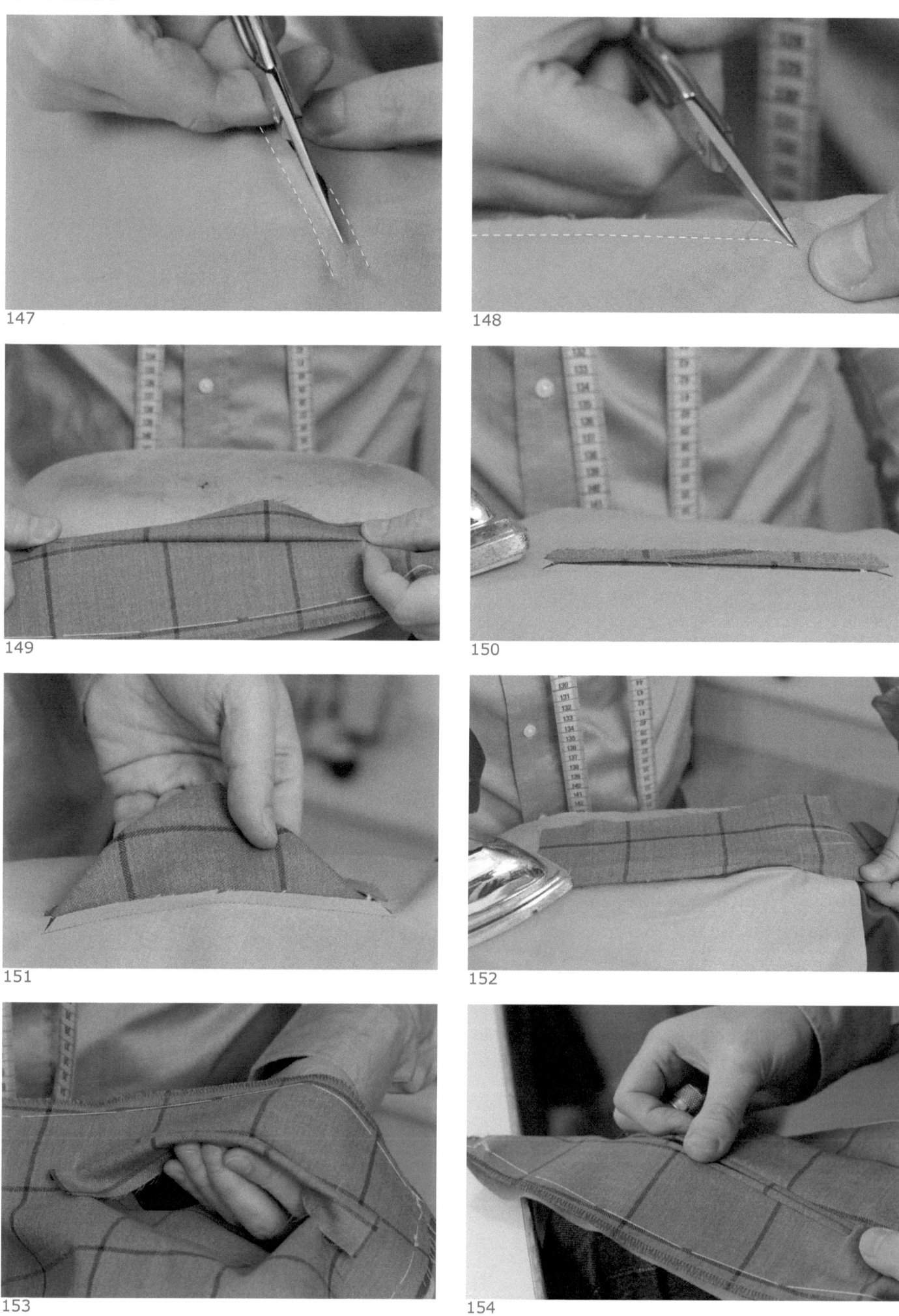

147

148

149

150

151

152

153

154

Cut open the pocket opening
Pictures 147/148
Now, the pocket opening is carefully cut open. At the ends of the opening, cut in the shape of a triangle as close to the seam as possible, just before the end of the last stitch. Attention, the seam allowance of the jet is not cut but pushed to the side!

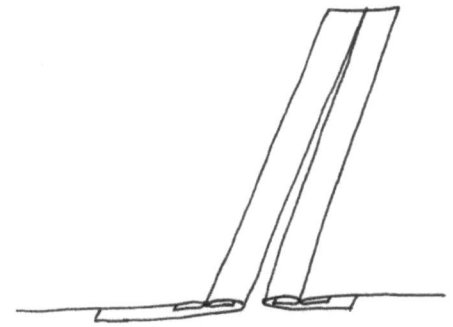

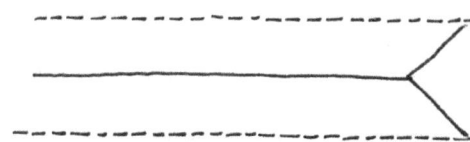

Then, the jets are sewn by hand with a point stitch precisely in the seam shadow. The jet width is shaped with the left hand and should be absolutely even, each for itself and both with each other. The width is approx. 0.5 cm, more usually looks chunky and less too filigree.

In any case, both jets together must be as wide as the distance between the two seams.

Press open the seam allowances
Picture 149
The front trousers are held so that the back jet hangs down (you can also fold down the jet with your fingers). Now, the entire part is carefully pulled onto the iron pad.

Picture 150
This means the rear jet is folded over, and the seam allowance can be pressed open.
The front jet should lie completely flat.
Attention must be paid to precise work at the corners. This will make it easier to hand-sew the jets.

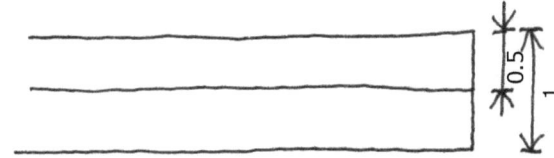

Pictures 151/152
Now, the front jet is pulled through the pocket opening, and the seam allowance is carefully pressed open.

Basting together the jets
Picture 154
Now the jets are basted together. In the case of a fabric pattern, it must be taken into account.

Hand sewing the jets
Picture 153
Then, the rear jet is pushed through the pocket opening. After everything has been ironed flat properly, the jets can be folded. The seam allowance of the jets disappears into the formed jet.

155

156

157

158

159

160

161

162

Picture 155

Both jets should match exactly in the fabric pattern. Then, the corners can be carefully pushed inwards with the scissors. (See picture 99 on page 42.)

Securing the corners

Picture 156

Now, the corners are secured with the sewing machine. Particular care should be taken here, as otherwise, the corners can fray later.
The sewing machine needle is inserted precisely in the corner; then, it is sewn to the other corner, reverse and forward again.

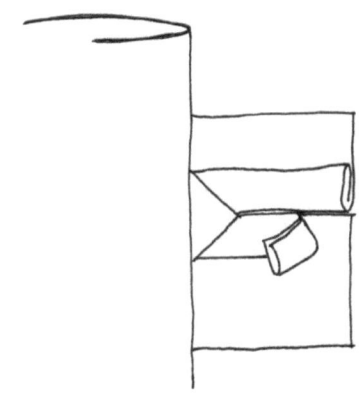

Picture 159

The front jet is now folded at the lower edge and ironed flat. Then, a piece of cardboard is placed under the pocket bag, and the jet is basted on.

The facing

Picture 160

The pocket facing is folded in at the front, ironed flat and then placed, with the right sides together, onto the pocket opening. The facing should reach above the pocket opening at the top and the end of the pocket bag at the bottom.

Picture 161

Now, close the pocket bag, slide one hand under the front trousers and place the other hand on the pocket bag. Press the trousers tightly between your hands and carefully turn them over so the facing does not slip.

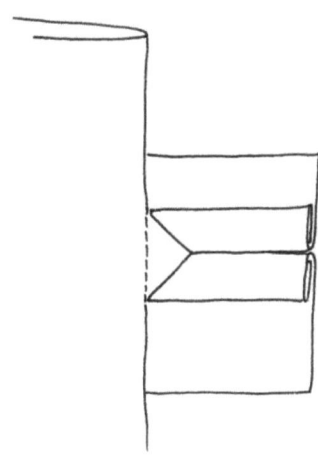

Picture 157

Then, the front jet is sewn from the back, which makes it more durable. To do this, lay open the pocket bag with the inside to the table and make sure that the jet with the pocket bag is on the right and the rest of the front trousers on the left of the sewing machine needle. (The picture is mirrored because we look at the sewing machine from behind). Only the front jet is stitched to the pocket bag. The outer fabric remains completely untouched.

Grading down the jets

Picture 158

Now, the jets are graded down. Two layers are cut away on the inside. So, less can bulge through to the outside.

Picture 162

Unfold the pocket bag and attach the facing. Trim the facing and the front jet at the lower edge of the pocket bag by approximately 0.75 cm to ensure a neat and tidy finish. Secure the facing and the front jet to the pocket bag using pins or basting stitches.
Now, the facing and the front jet can be sewn onto the pocket bag.

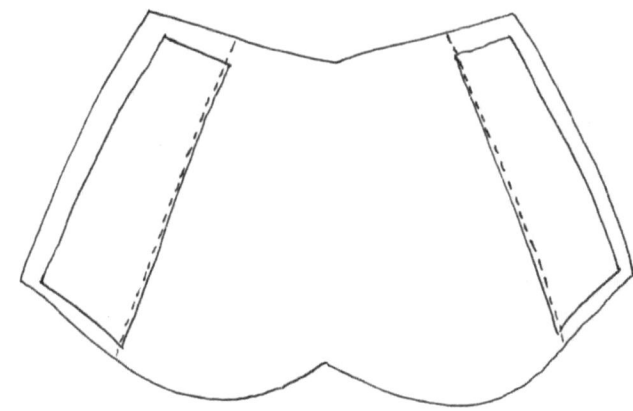

163

164

165

166

167

168

169

170

Closing the pocket bag

Picture 163

Now, place the pocket bag right sides together at the fold line and close with a seam.

Picture 164

Since the lower part of the pocket bag is cut in bias, care must be taken that it is not stretched and that the pocket bag fits together precisely.

Picture 165

Now, the pocket bag is turned inside out, and the corner is worked out nicely with an awl or the folding bone. The seam allowances of the pocket bag, the jets, and the facing should lie smooth.

Picture 166

The pocket bag is now sewn on, again with a seam of 0.75 cm, so it is neatened on the inside, and no seam allowances are exposed.
Ensure that every single layer inside the bag is in its place.

Securing the back jet

Pictures 167/168/169

Then, the rear jet is secured while the pocket bag is closed at the back. The upper part of the pocket bag, the rear jet and the lower part of the pocket bag are connected to one another. Stitch on the pocket bag, just next to the seam, and make sure that nothing is shifted while sewing. Thus, the rear jet is also fixed and more durable.

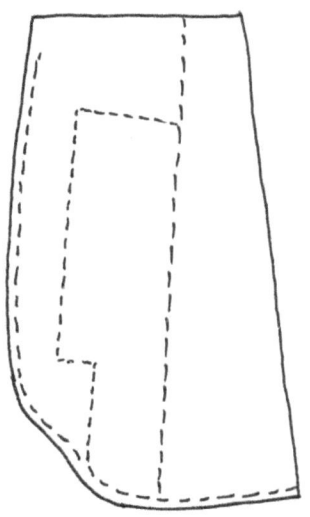

Picture 170

Now, everything can be pressed nicely; even the pocket bag is ironed again.

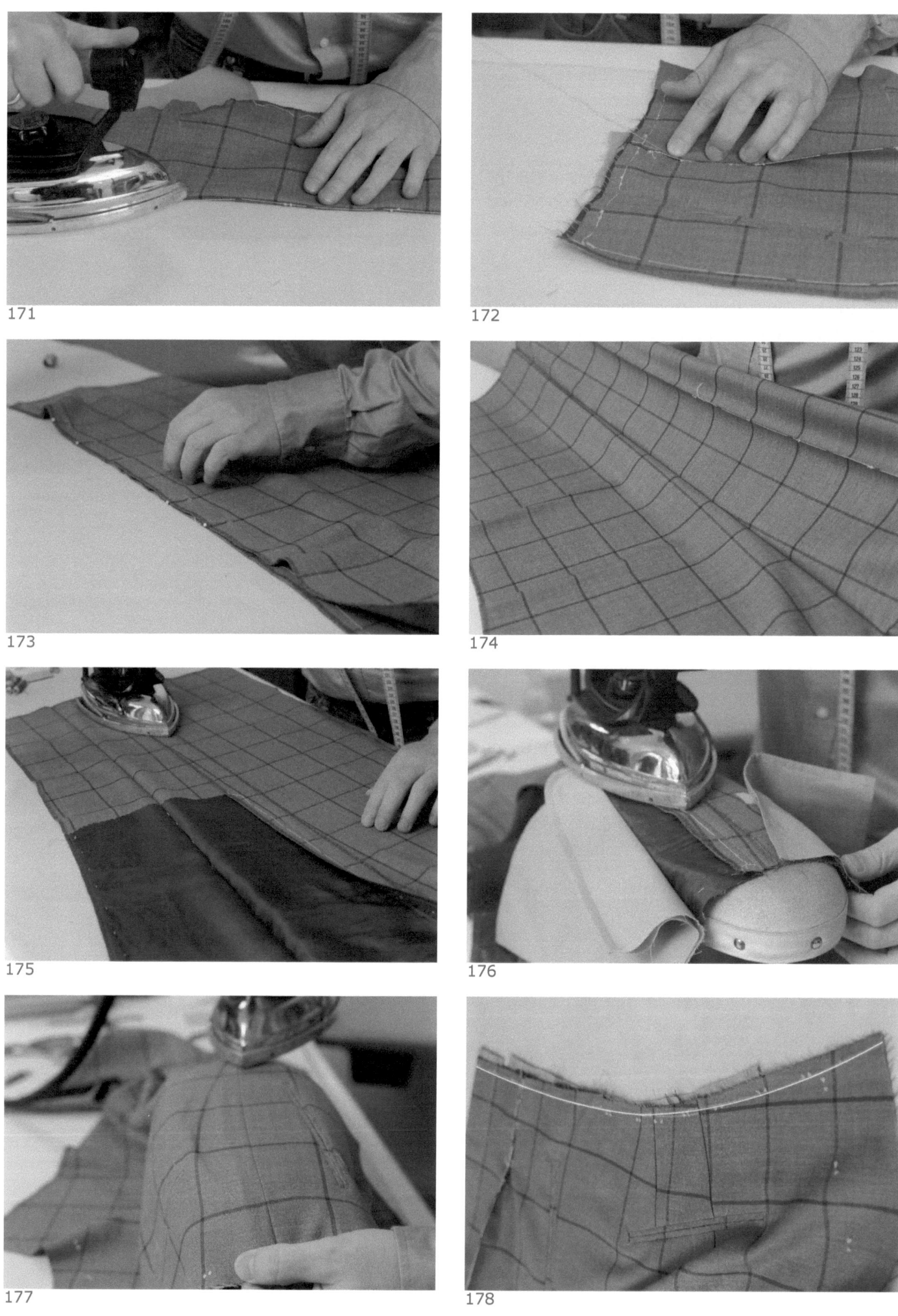

171

172

173

174

175

176

177

178

Pressing the front trousers

Picture 171

Fold the front trousers precisely at the breakline and iron them evenly.

Picture 172

Fold over the break at the waistband, create a pleat and baste down approximately 5 cm.

Assembling the sideseam

Picture 173

Place the back trousers onto the front trousers at the side seam and fix with pins.

Picture 174

If the fabric has a pattern, the entire side seam must fit. Now, the side seam is sewn with 2 cm seam allowance (or as much as you left when cutting). This is essential to ensure that the pattern does not shift.

Picture 175

First, check whether the seam runs evenly and the pattern fits together. Then, the seam allowance can be pressed open.

Picture 176

Because of the hip arch, it is advisable to iron flat the upper part of the side seam using an ironing pad.

Picture 177

Then, the seam can be carefully pressed from the right side.

Leveling out the waistband-line

Picture 178

It is important to lay flat the trousers' upper front and back and ensure the waistband-seam-line is levelled out. This step is especially necessary with back darts in order to achieve a smooth and polished appearance.

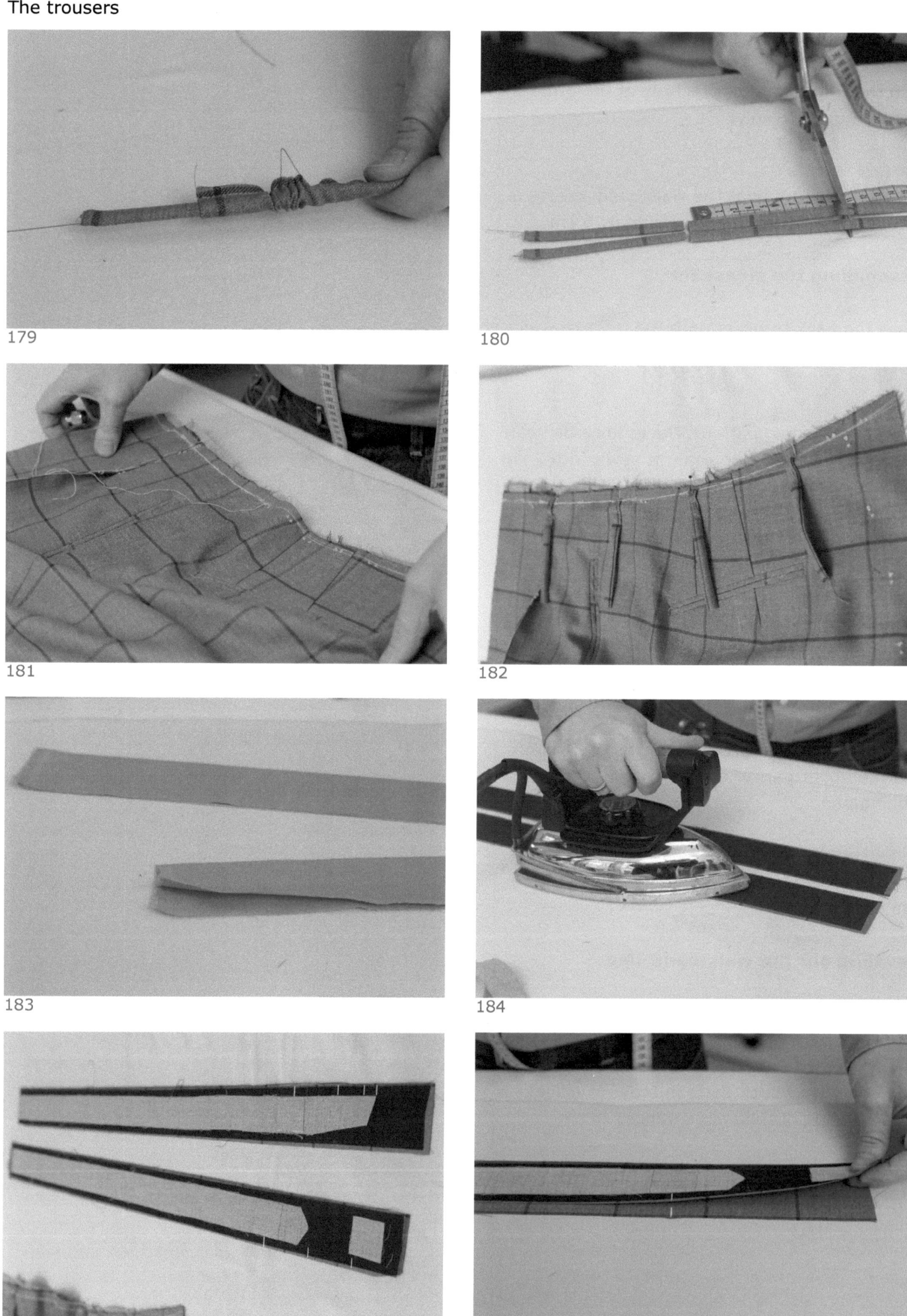

179

180

181

182

183

184

185

186

The belt loops

Picture 179

The belt loops are sewn by a width of approximately 1 cm.
A buttonhole thread is sewn on well at one end with a thick needle and then pulled through the belt loop. Make sure that the thread does not crack while turning the belt loops inside out.

Picture 180

All the belt loops should look even when using a fabric with a pattern. Eight loops, each approximately 9 cm long, are required.

Attaching the pocket bags

Picture 181

Now, the pocket bags are fixed at the top of the waistband seam. Make sure that they lie flat and do not warp the outer fabric.

Picture 182

Then, the belt loops can be attached. The first loop is placed exactly on the crease line, the last with a distance of approximately 5.5 cm to the center back. For the remaining loops, the distance between both loops is divided into three.

Picture 183

The waistband lining is folded up lengthwise, with the wrong sides facing together and ironed flat.

Stiffening the waistband

Picture 184

First, press on a thin, fusible interlining to the waistband.

Cutting the waistband interlining

Adhesive horsehair is particularly suitable as a waistband insert. The width corresponds to the waistband's width minus approximately 2 mm (see explanation on page 33).
The length is 1/2 of the waistband's length plus approximately 15 cm. The horsehair thread should run horizontally, from top to bottom, not from front to back. This allows the horsehair's elasticity to keep the waistband stable.
Alternatively, a simple, solid adhesive fabric insert can be used.

The adhesive horsehair should be wetted with lukewarm water and dried beforehand. This will prevent it from shrinking later. Because of the adhesive particles, be careful not to iron it dry.

Picture 185

Then, the fusible horsehair is ironed onto the inner waistband straight and evenly.
When sewing on the right waistband, leave open the seam at the 2-cm-marking for the counter button.

Waistband right

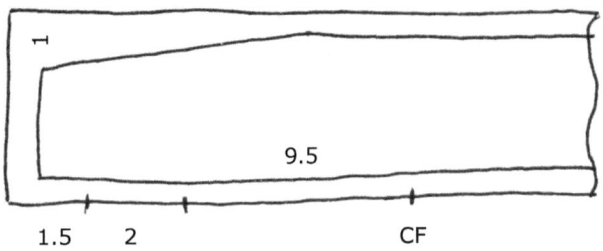

Waistband left

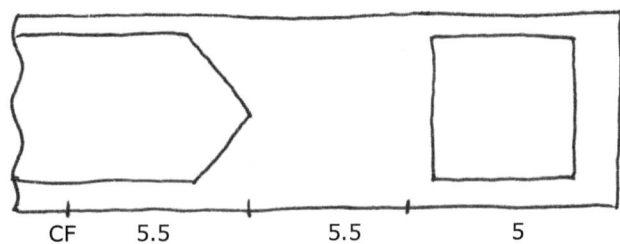

A piece of fusible horsehair is ironed onto the left waistband. This serves as reinforcement so that the hook will hold properly later and not tear out easily.

Picture 186

Place the right and left waistbands on top of each other and mark the center front. For fabrics with a pattern, this should run evenly from the center front to the center back.

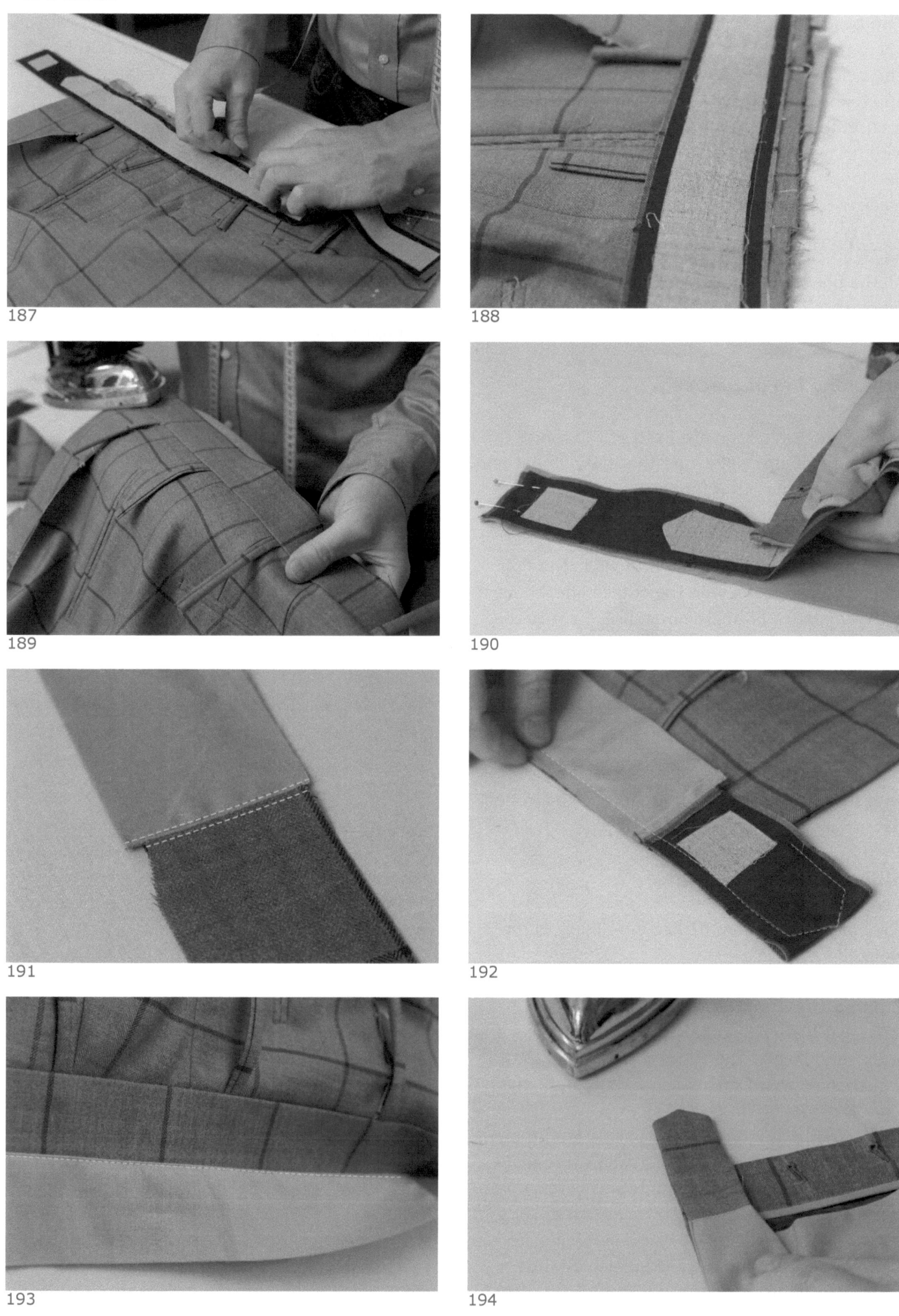

187

188

189

190

191

192

193

194

The left waistband

Picture 187
Pin on the waistband, starting at the center front.

Picture 188
Now, the waistband is sewn by approx. 2 mm next to the edge of the horsehair. The pocket bags, the knee lining and the fold, should be noted so everything is in place correctly.

Picture 189
Iron flat the waistband at the left front trousers.

Picture 190
The waistband lining was folded lengthwise in the middle and ironed flat. Now, secure the waistband lining with the open edge facing up and the fold facing down. Then, sew on the waistband lining.

Picture 191
The waistband and the waistband lining are ironed flat and evenly secured with a seam at both sides. Then, fold over the waistband at the waistband extension and secure it with pins.

Picture 192
Sew on the waistband lining at the left front trousers. Start from the center back to the front, around the tip and to the edge of the fly. The seam should be approx. 2 mm from the edge of the horsehair.

Picture 193
Then, fold over the waistband lining and topstitch by approximately 1 mm (on the waistband lining).
At the end of the waistband, where the folded fabric of the waistband extension begins, the seam ends and is locked.

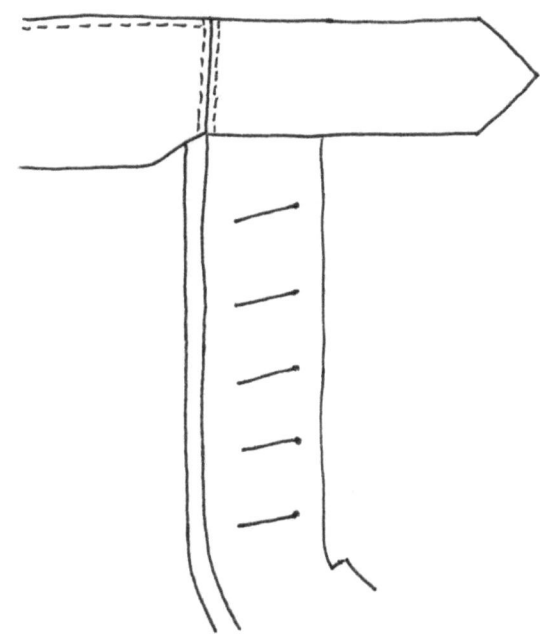

Picture 194
At the left front trousers, work out the tip of the waistband extension with an awl or the folding bone and iron flat.

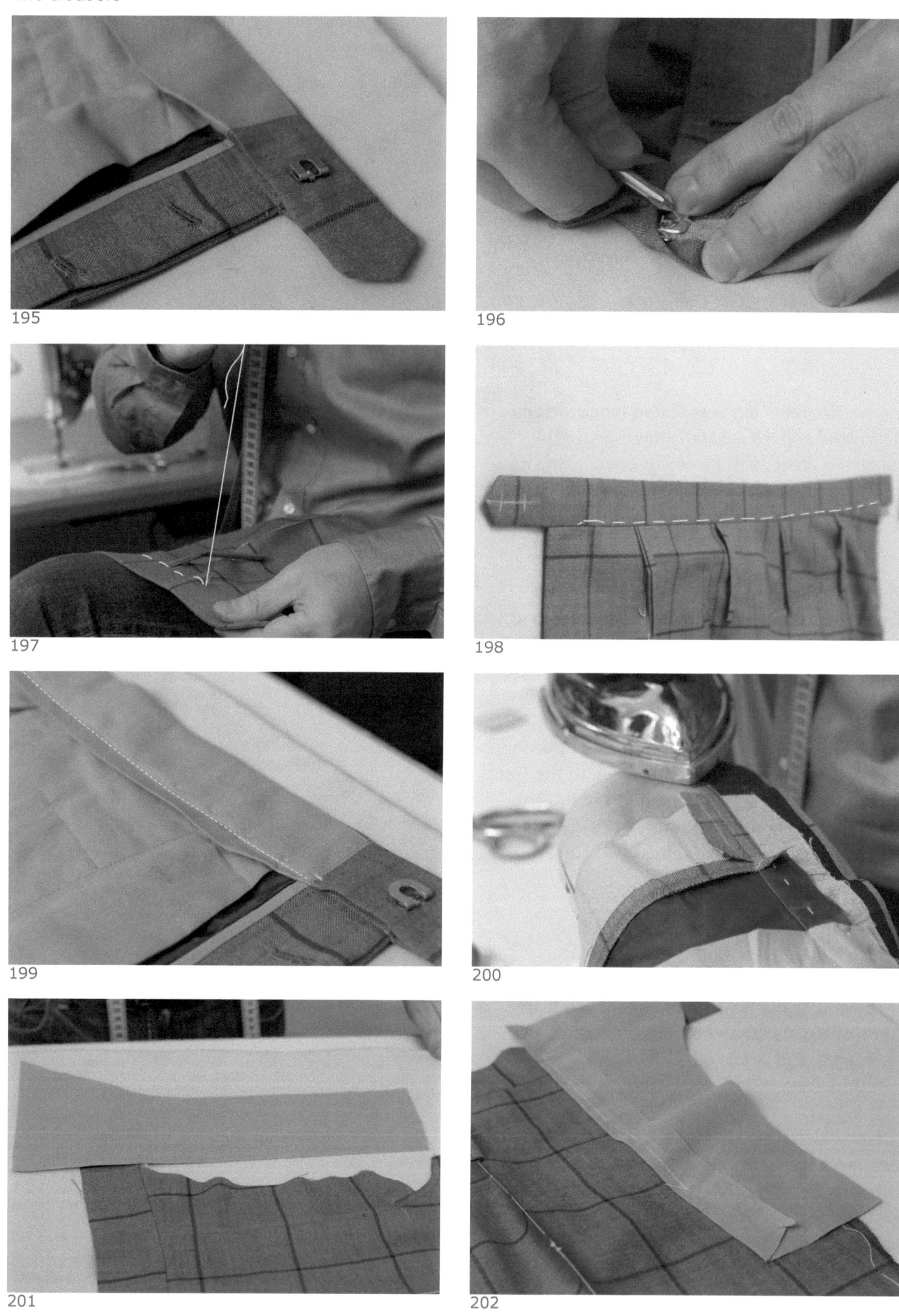

195

196

197

198

199

200

201

202

The hook

Picture 195

A hook to press in is the best option.

First, fold away the lining. Place the hook on the left waistband in the direction of the fly's edge and push the thorns through the inner waistband.

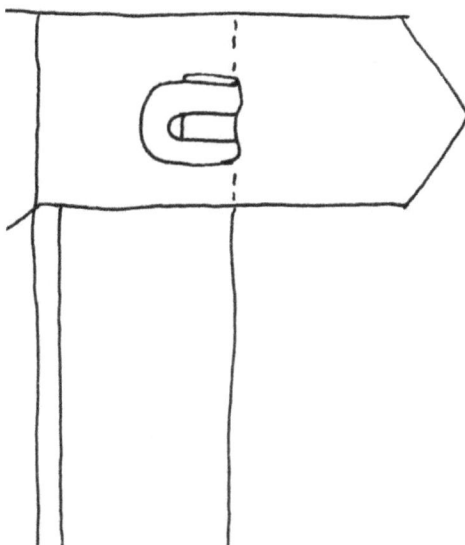

If a hook with eyelets is used, it is sewn at the desired position.

Picture 196

Place the counterpart for the hook on the inside and carefully bend the thorns with a Phillips screwdriver. A standard screwdriver is more dangerous to slip off. There is also an apparatus for bending the thorns, but it is pretty expensive and unnecessary.

Basting the waistband

Picture 197

Now, fold back the waistband lining of the left front trousers and attach it to the waistband from the outside with basting stitches.

The buttonhole at the waistband extension

Picture 198

Mark the buttonhole on the waistband extension and topstitch with tiny stitches.

Then, topstitch the waistband right beside the waistline seam, directly under the waistband. Start from the front at the fly seam and move to the center back.

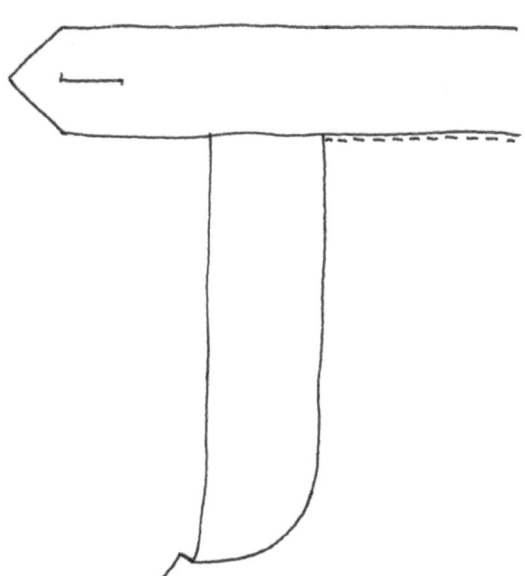

Picture 199

The short gap that is still open at the inside of the waistband will be closed by hand later (see picture 225 on page 72).

The right waistband

As with the left front trousers, the belt loops are attached first. Now, the waistband is pinned, starting at the center front. Then, top stitch approximately 2 mm beside the horsehair edge from back to front and iron flat (Attention: Don't forget the buttonhole in the seam).

The fly extension

Picture 200

At the center front, the waistband seam is pressed open (seam allowance ironed to both sides).

Picture 201

Now, a piece of pocket lining is folded by approximately 2 cm and ironed flat. Then, it is placed on the fly seam, covering the seam by approximately 1 cm.

Picture 202

The lining for the fly extension must protrude a little over the waistband and cover the entire fly extension at the bottom. Later, the seam allowance should also be covered on the fly.

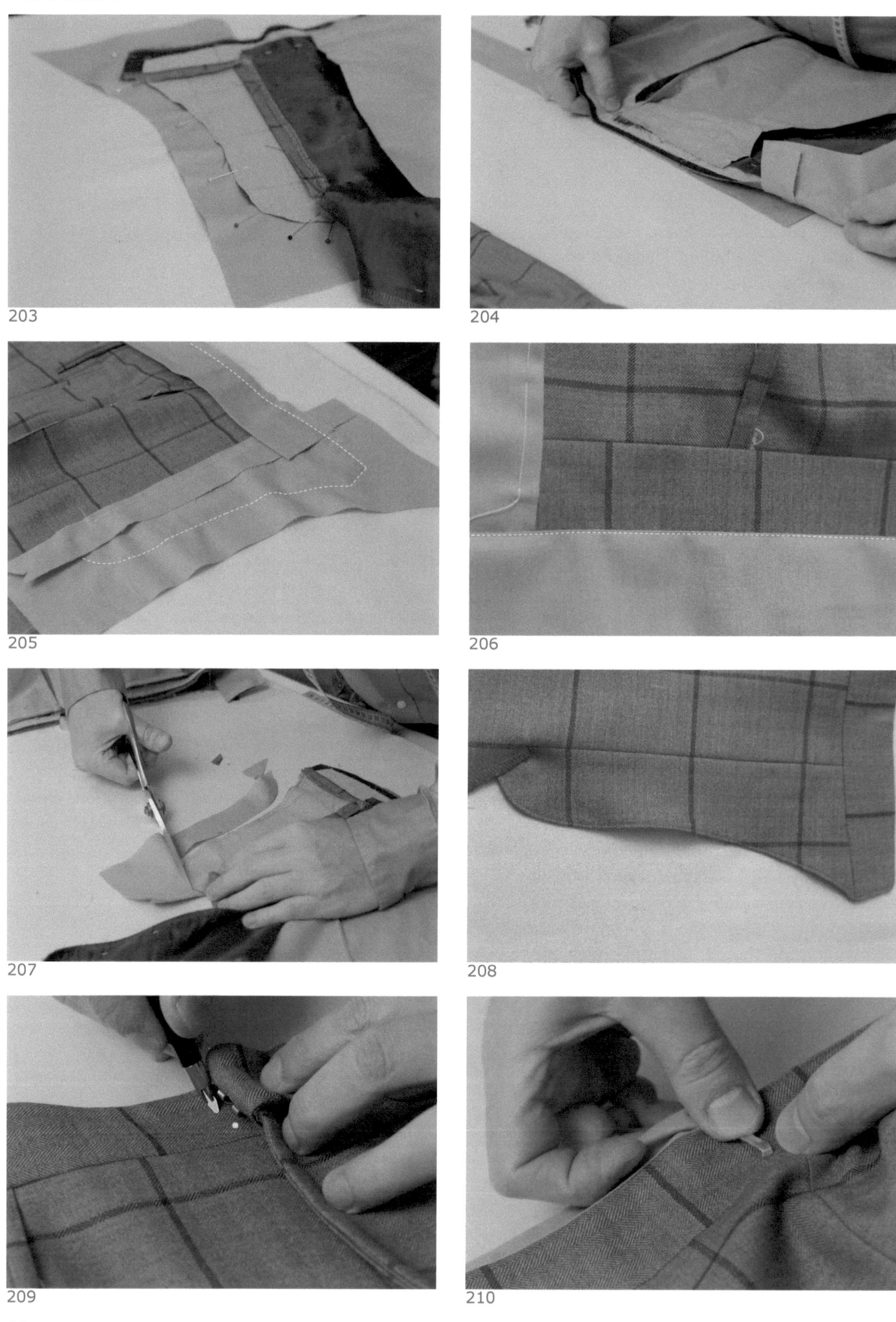

203

204

205

206

207

208

209

210

The fly extension

Picture 203

The fly extension can now be turned over, and the lining can be pinned on.

Picture 204

Then, the folded waistband lining (with the opening edges pointing up and the fold pointing down) is pinned in place and sewn on.
It should protrude about 4 cm above the lining from the fly extension.

Picture 205

Now, the fly extension and waistband lining are attached. Sew at the waistband, like on the left side, about 2 mm beside the horsehair edge.

Picture 206

Then, the waistband lining is stitched flat by approximately 1 mm.

Picture 207

Now, cut back the lining of the fly extension.

Picture 208

Turn the fly extension inside out, iron flat, and then topstitch it with a narrow seam.

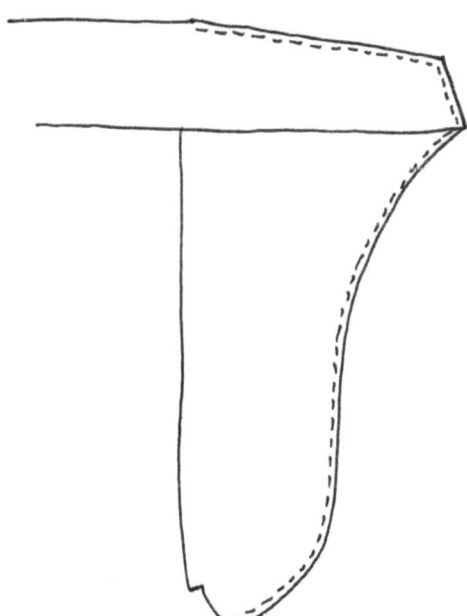

The eyelet for the hook

Picture 209

Place the left front trousers on top of the right (pay attention to the fabric's pattern) and mark the position of the eyelet for the hook with a chalk pen on the right front trousers.

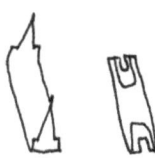

Picture 210

The eyelet is now just pressed in, while the waistband lining is folded away.

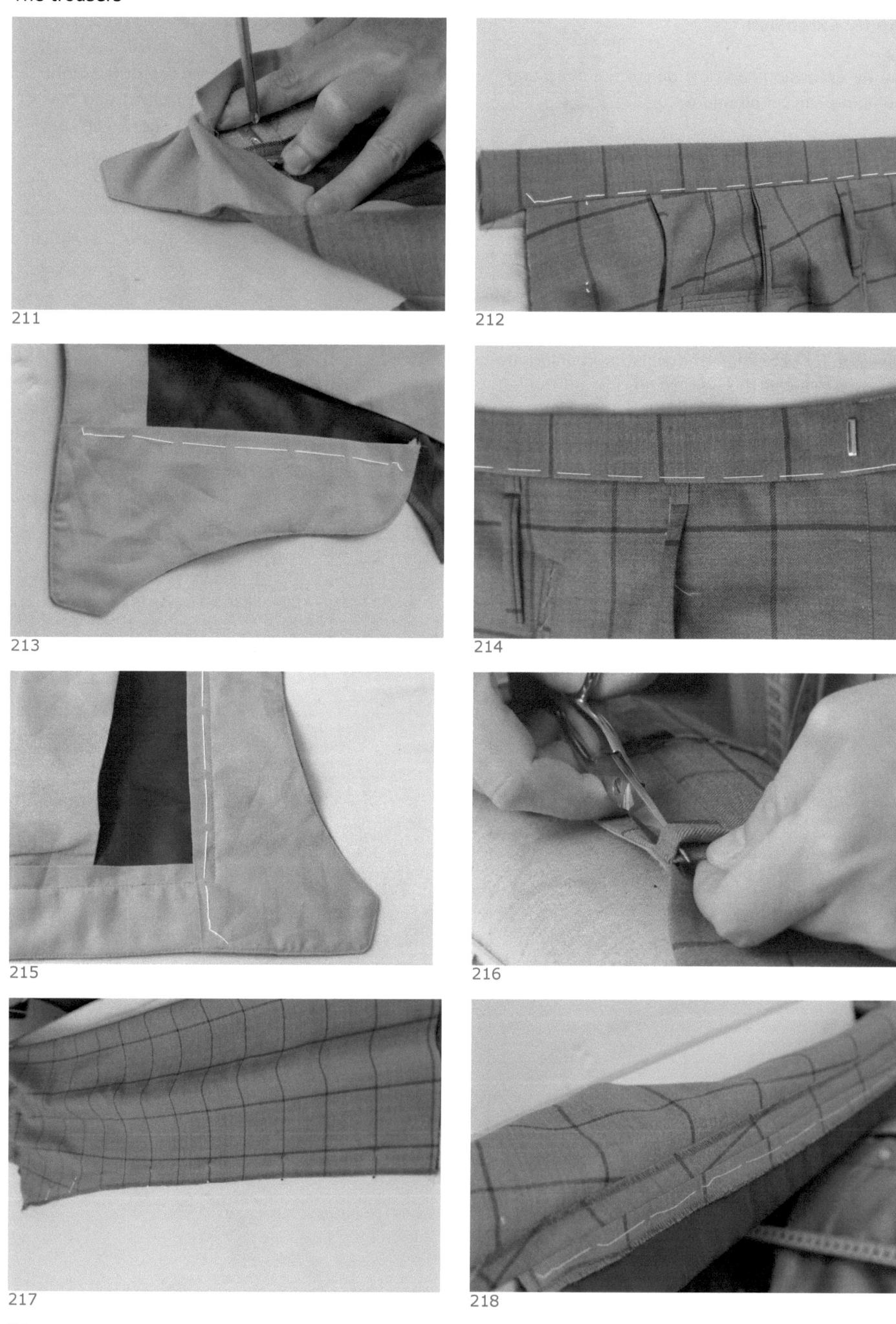

211

212

213

214

215

216

217

218

The eyelet for the hook

Picture 211

The eyelet is secured from the inside with the counterpart. The thorns are carefully bent over with the Phillips screwdriver.
Attention: Too many attempts to bend back and forth cause the thorns to break off very quickly.

The waistband lining and the fly extension

Picture 212

Now, the waistband lining of the right front trousers is turned inside and basted to the waistband from front to back.

Picture 213

On the inside, baste down the fly extension's lining, ensuring that the seam allowance of the fly seam is covered.

The belt loops

Picture 214

The belt loops are fixed by approximately 1 cm below the waistband. Ensure that the waistband lining on the inside is folded away and that everything is flat and not warped.

The waistband lining of the right front trousers is sewn on just below the waistband seam; then, from the hook down, the fly extension lining is sewn on at the front trousers, just next to the fly seam.

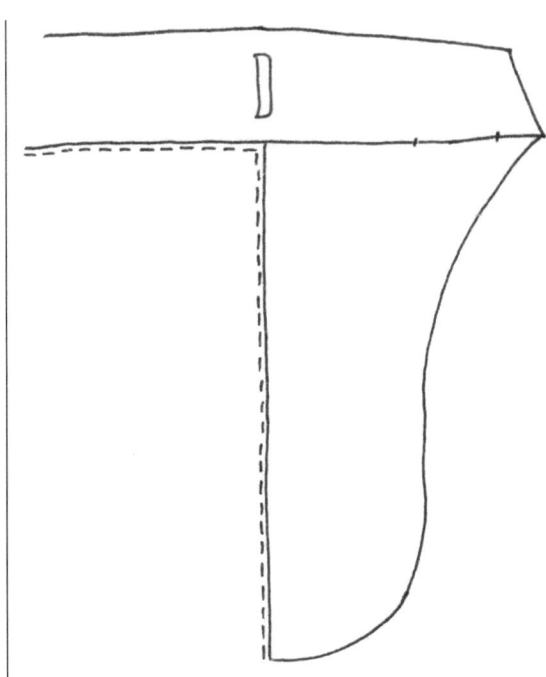

Picture 215

The reverse side of the seam should also be checked here.
Then, the belt loops are turned upward, tucked in at the top of the waistband, and sewn. They should be a little loose and without tension.

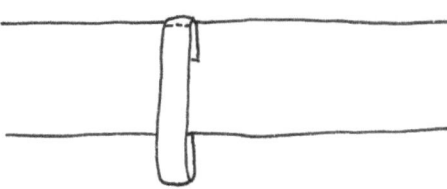

Picture 216

The excess material of the belt loops is now carefully cut away.

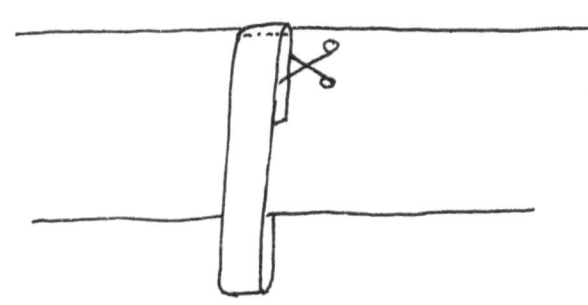

Closing the inside seam

Picture 217

Place the back trousers on the front and fix them with pins. The fabric pattern must fit from the knee point down to the hem.
Now, the inside seam is sewn at the back trousers with 2 cm seam allowance (or as much as you left when cutting). It is important to ensure that the fabric pattern does not shift.

Picture 218

First, check whether the seam runs evenly and the fabric pattern fits together. Then, the seam allowance can be pressed open.
Because the back trousers have been stretched in the upper part of the inside seam, the pattern from the knee point towards the seat seam no longer matches. That is absolutely correct.

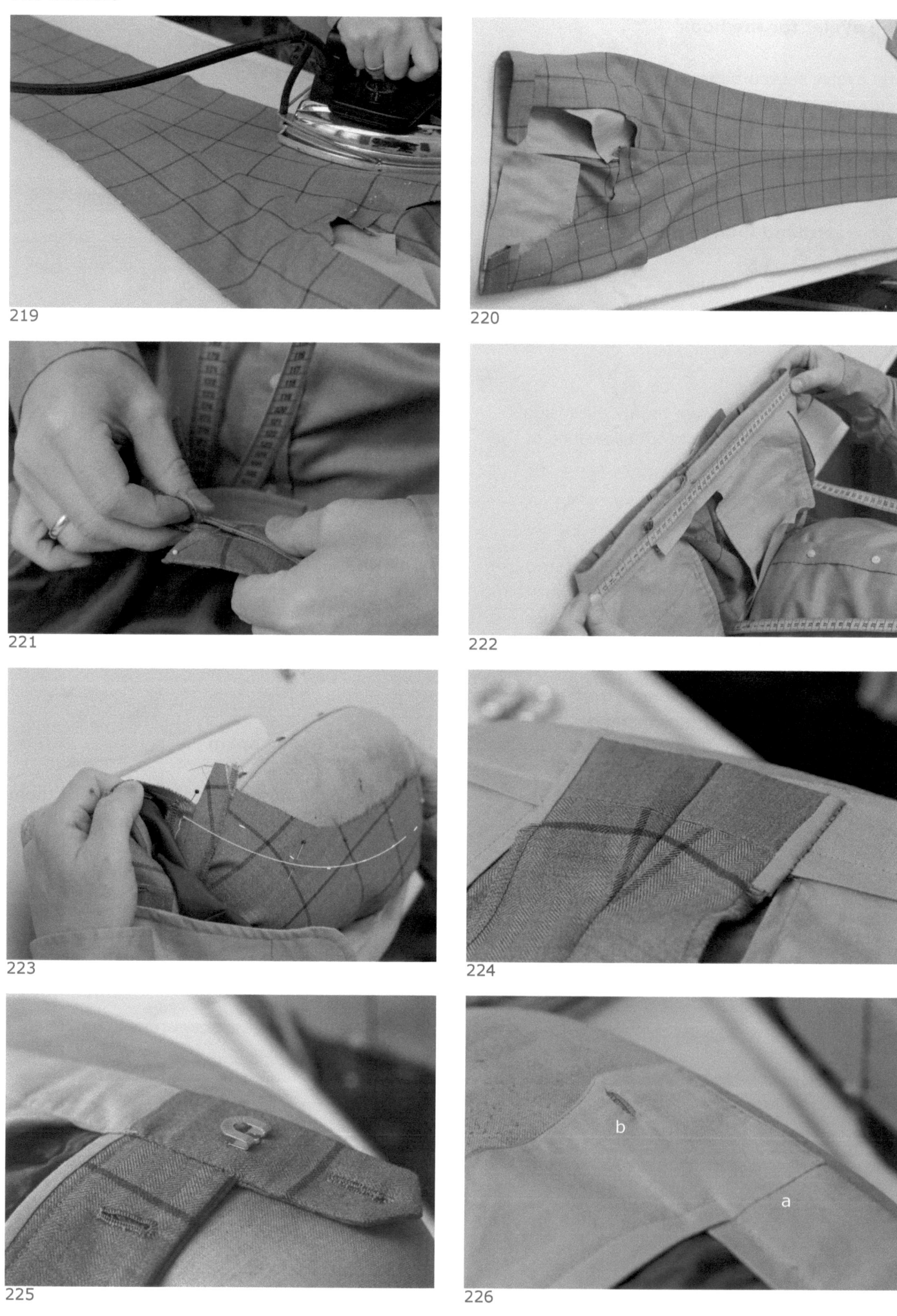

219

220

221

222

223

224

225

226

back break

Pictures 219/220

Both trousers' legs are turned right side out, laid flat and pressed at the back break.
If the trousers have a fabric pattern, they are now ironed into shape. The back of the trousers is stretched in the calf area, and the front is kept short on the tibia. The fabric on the back trousers is also kept short under the seat.

Picture 221

Now, turn the right trousers' leg inside out again. Then, push the left trousers' leg into the right one and pin the seat seam together. Pay attention to the fabric pattern as well.

Controlling the waistband width

Picture 222

The waistband is first put together with just one needle. Then, the trousers' hook is closed, and the width is checked and adjusted if necessary.

The seat seam

Picture 223

The course of the seat seam is remarked and then sewn from the fly to the back. After checking the seam and the fabric pattern, the seat seam should be sewn a second time. Meanwhile, the fabric is stretched slightly, making the seam more elastic and stable.

The seam allowance of the seat seam is cut to size. Approximately 2 cm in the arch and approximately 5 cm at the waistband should be enough. Then, the seam is serged with the overlock sewing machine. The lower part of the seat seam is stretched with the iron (where the crosses are), and then the seam allowance is pressed open.

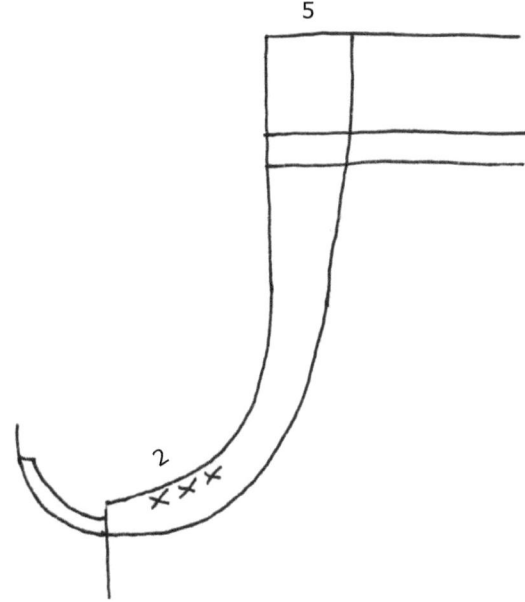

Picture 224

The upper back part of the waistband is bound and fixed to the waistband with buttonhole thread.
Alterations in the width can be made faster, and it still looks neatly tailored.

Picture 225

The open part of the inner waistband at the left fly is sewn with buttonhole thread.
Once the zipper has been sewn in, carefully push the end into the open part of the waistband. This area is then closed by hand with a blind stitch. (See page 114, picture 372 for reference)

The buttonholes

Now, the buttonholes at the back pockets and the waistband extension are hand-sewn.
(See page 51)

Picture 226

The open part at the right side of the inner waistband is closed with a blind stitch (a).
For the counter button's buttonhole, the lining is incised, turned inside a little, and blind-stitched twice all around (b).

227

228

229

230

231

232

233

234

The blind hem

Picture 227

The length of the trousers is measured and marked on the inside leg, from the crotch down to the hem. It's better to measure twice than cut off and be too short.

Picture 228

The length can be straight or at a slight angle, as desired. The hem allowance should be approximately 6 cm. To prevent bulging on the right side, the hem is not trimmed with an overlock sewing machine but cut off with pinking scissors.

Preparing the kicktape

The 3 cm wide kicktape is folded over by 0.75 cm on both sides, one after the other and sewn flat.

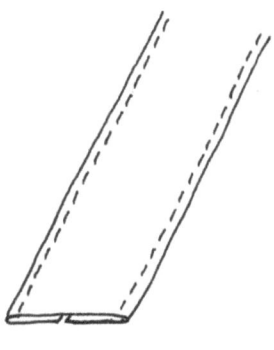

Alternatively, of course, a finished kick tape can be used. However, this is usually very stiff and will never fit perfectly in terms of colour.

Picture 229

After the trousers' leg has been turned inside out, the kicktape can be sewn underneath the chalk line (*LG*). Then, the front part of the hem allowance is carefully stretched with the iron. This way, it does not pull at the front trousers after it has been fixed up with a hemstitch.

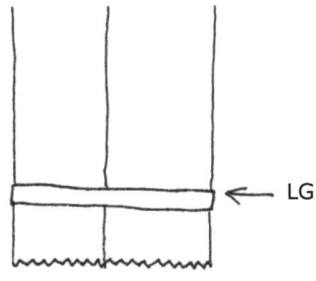

Picture 230

The hem allowance is turned inside and fixed with basting thread. The kicktape should be visible by 1 mm; this is how it serves its purpose best.

Picture 231

The hem allowance is fixed with a blind hemstitch. Ensure that only a few threads are picked up with the needle and that the stitch is not pulled too tight so that the stitches are invisible on the right side.

Pressing the trousers

Picture 232

Now, the trousers are pressed with a heavy iron and an ironing cloth. This prevents the fabric from getting shiny.
First, iron the trousers' legs individually, at the inside and the outside seams. All remaining basting threads and tacking stitches are pulled out during this process.

Picture 233

Then, iron the pockets, the fly and everything else on the ironing pad.

Picture 234

The processing will be easier with tools: the trousers' hook is inserted into a thick cardboard template with a slot. Then, the left waistband is flat and easy to iron.

After pressing, the trousers should be carefully hung up on a trousers hanger and allowed to cool. This prevents the trousers from forming new wrinkles or folds.

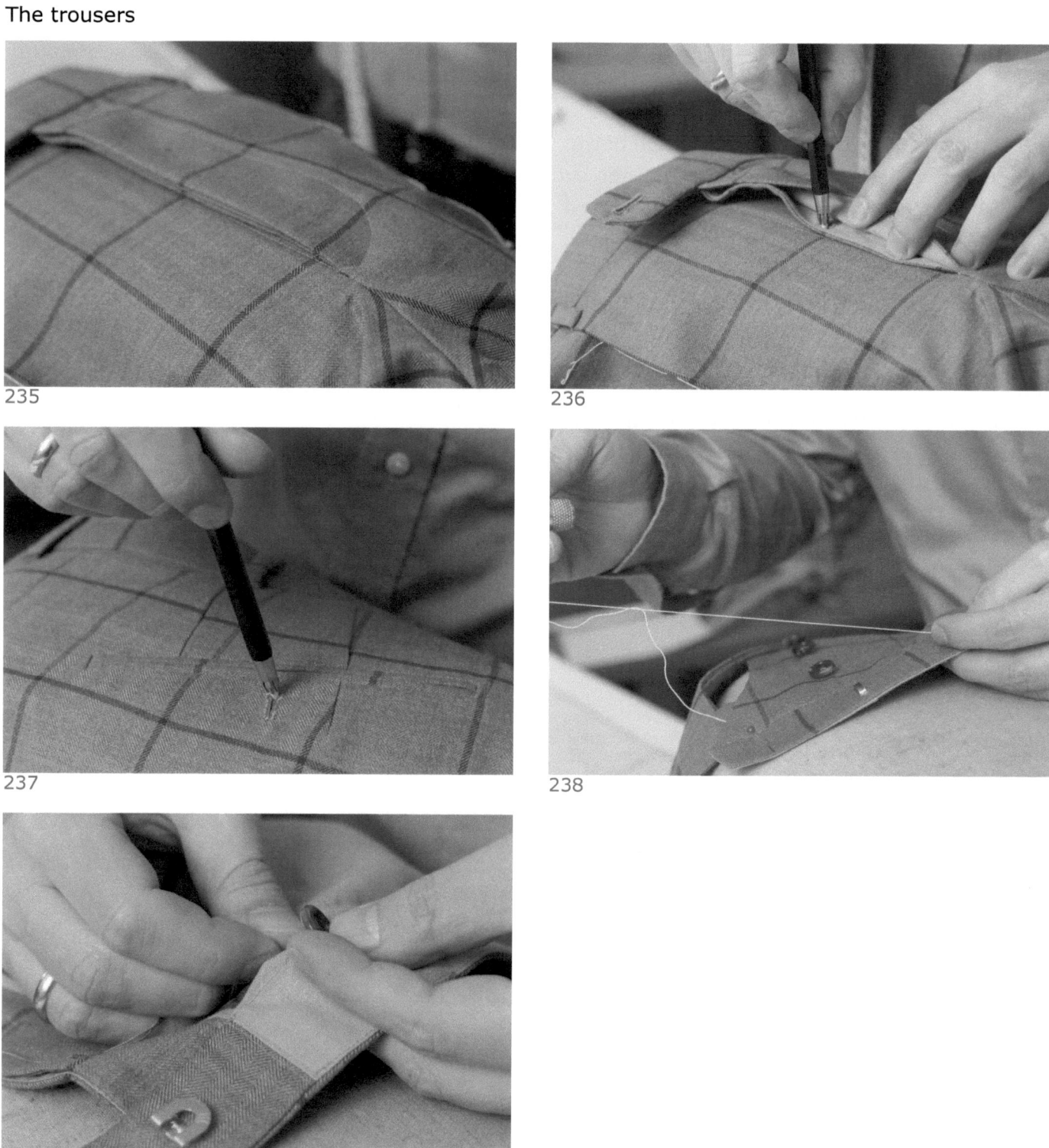

235

236

237

238

239

Marking the buttons

Pictures 235/236

When the trousers have cooled down, the positions of the buttons are marked.
Put the fly together as desired, carefully fold back the upper part and mark through the holes with the chalk pen.

Picture 237

The same is done with the back pocket, the waistband extension and the counter button.

Sewing on the buttons

Pictures 238/239

Then, all buttons are carefully sewn on with waxed buttonhole thread and a short stem. The buttonhole silk is pulled over a beeswax candle and then placed between a folded piece of blotting paper and ironed off.
Ensure no beeswax crumbs end on the trousers and cause stains.
When sewing, the thread "sticks," and the button will not come off easily.

Of course, it is advisable to ensure that the trousers remain wrinkle-free.

240

Link to the
vest videos

https://www.becomeatailor.com/videos-waistcoat/

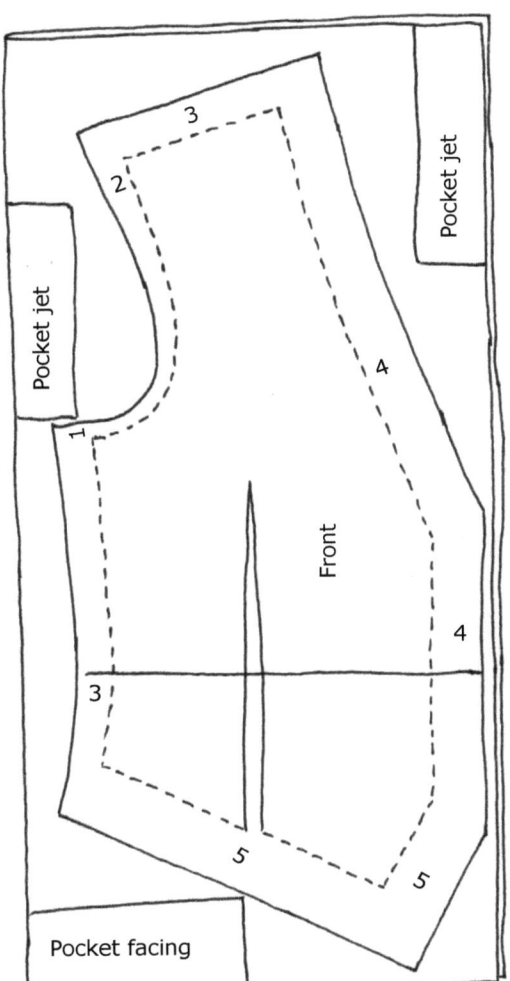

Cutting the front part of the vest

You should also pay attention to the grainline for the vest. Simply breathe into your hand and stroke it over the fabric. With some practice, you can feel the grainline and recognize the pile direction. The vest is cut in the same grainline as the matching trousers. Otherwise, the fabric can shimmer slightly lighter or darker. The seam allowances are marked as shown in the sketch. Otherwise, at least a seam allowance of 0.75 or 1 cm is marked everywhere else (see also explanation on page 127).

Dimensions for the pockets

Facing: width approx. 15 cm,
length approx. 5 cm

Jets: width approx. 5 cm,
length approx. 15 cm

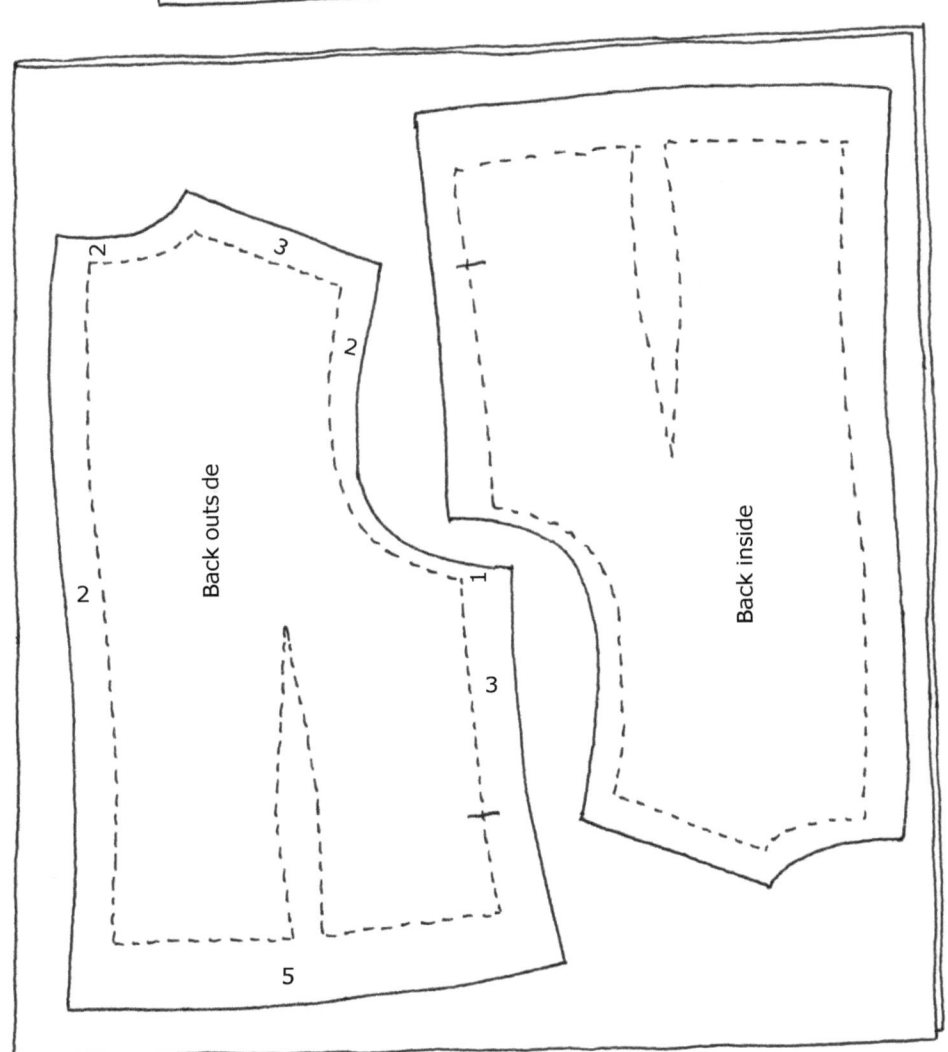

Cutting the back of the vest

If the vest's back is made of lining material, it can be cut upside down. There is no grain direction or pile.

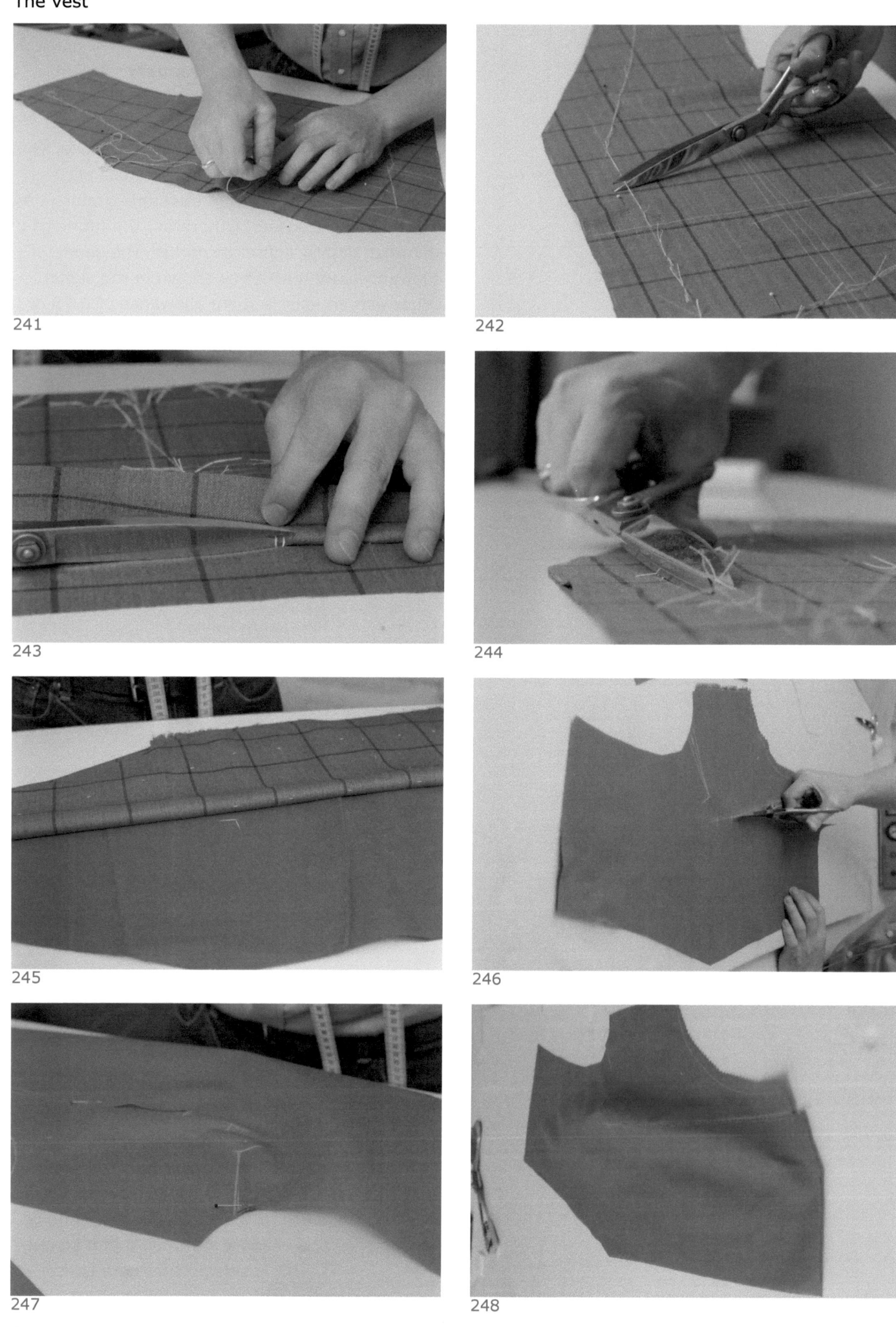

241

242

243

244

245

246

247

248

Tacking

Picture 241

Both front parts are put on top of each other, facing the right sides together.

Make sure that the fabric pattern is precisely aligned. First, fix it with pins and then tack it with double thread (see page 10).

Picture 242

Now, the thread is cut open between the stitches. The scissors should be guided from the inside out. If the fabric is accidentally pinched, this should happen at the seam allowance to minimize any visible damage.

Picture 243

Then, carefully pull the fabrics apart and cut the stitches between the fabric layers. Again, be careful not to cut into the fabric!

Picture 244

Now, put both layers of fabric back on each other and trim off the protruding threads of the stitches. It is worth noting that the stitches should be tacked on every chalk line of the vest.

Cutting the canvas

Picture 245

Place the front part on a piece of Holland linen (or something similar) in the same grainline and roughly cut out.

Draw a mark with chalk at the armhole, at the strongest point of the curve.

Carefully fold over the front part and mark the position of the dart. The fabric must not slip.

Picture 246

Remark the waist dart and the dart at the armhole, then cut along the marked lines to open them up.

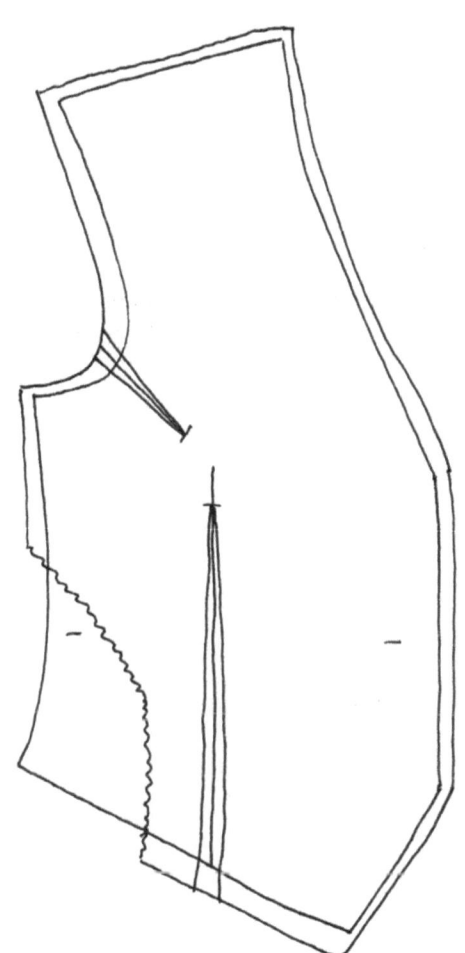

Shaping the canvas

Picture 247

Pin the darts in position and sew them together with a zig-zag stitch.

Picture 248

After sewing, the darts are ironed flat on the big ironing pad, allowing the inlay to be easily ironed into shape. A uniform bulge should be visible at the breast when the canvas is finished.

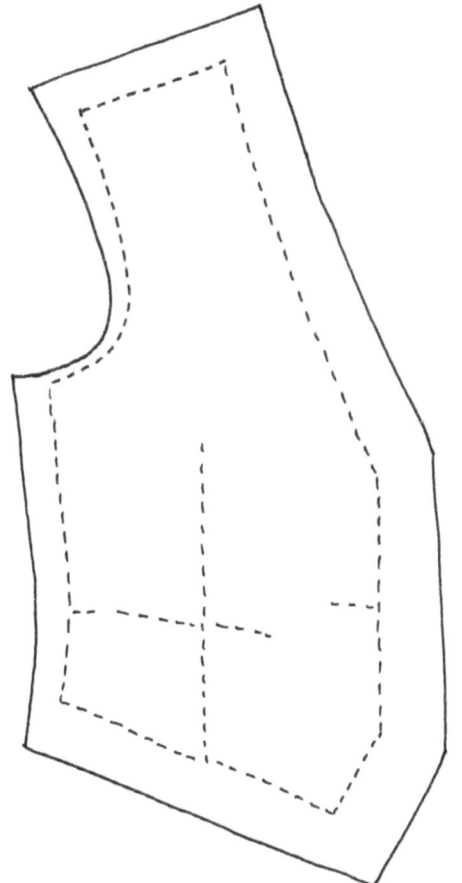

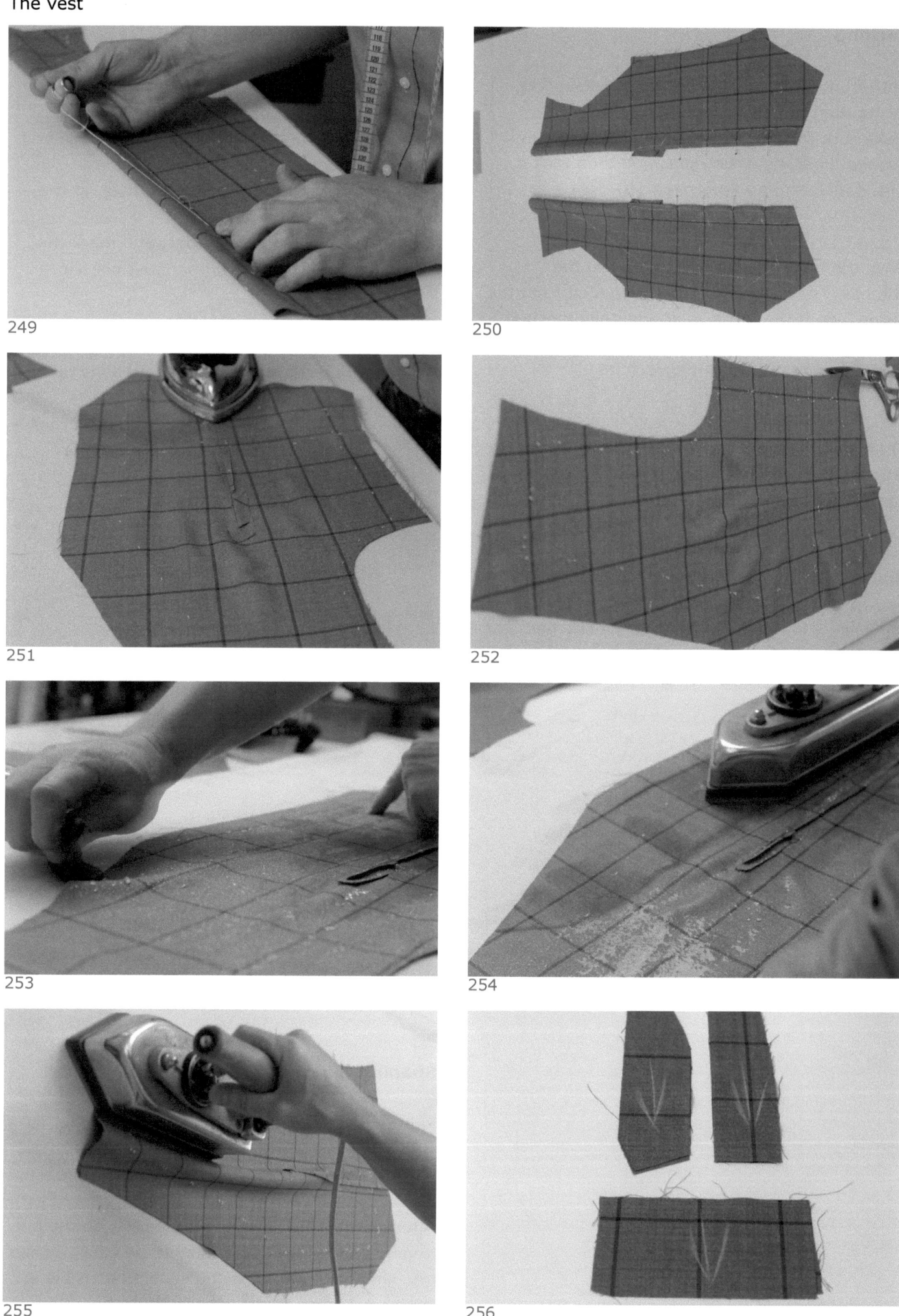

249

250

251

252

253

254

255

256

Closing the dart

The darts are basted so the fabric does not slip, and the pattern fits after sewing. Of course, the fabric pattern must match exactly.

Picture 250
The dart is folded and ironed flat. At the top of the dart point, an approximate 8 cm long piece of the same fabric, cut in bias, is placed underneath. This makes it easier to iron the tip. Additionally, the fabric pattern can also be secured with pins. Then, the darts are sewn.

Picture 251
The dart is carefully cut open up to the underlying fabric; then, the seam allowance of the dart is pressed open. The underlying piece at the top is cut away in stages.

Picture 252
The dart must be placed in the middle of the fabric pattern on both front pieces and should end at the same height. In the case of asymmetrical or continuous fabric patterns, the seam may have to be shifted and, therefore, might not be in the center.

Pressing the front

Picture 253
Now, the front part is pressed (ironed into shape). The crosses mean stretching, and the curved lines symbolize shrinking (keeping the area short).
With the right sides of the fabric facing each other, it ensures they are pressed evenly.
The front part is made wet with a cloth brush or a spray bottle.

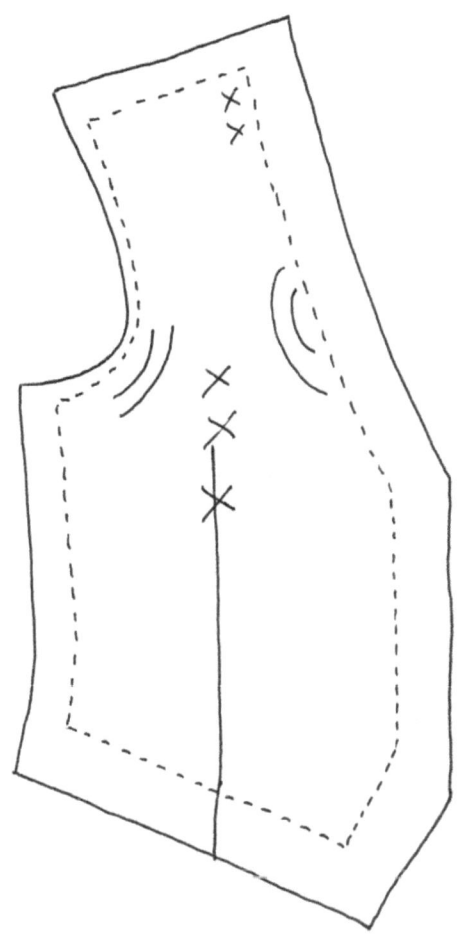

Picture 254
When dry ironing, the parts are also formed into shape.

Picture 255
The fabric pattern can be used as a guide. It should always be even and not warped.

Picture 256
The pieces for the jets and the pocket facing should also be made wet and then ironed dry.

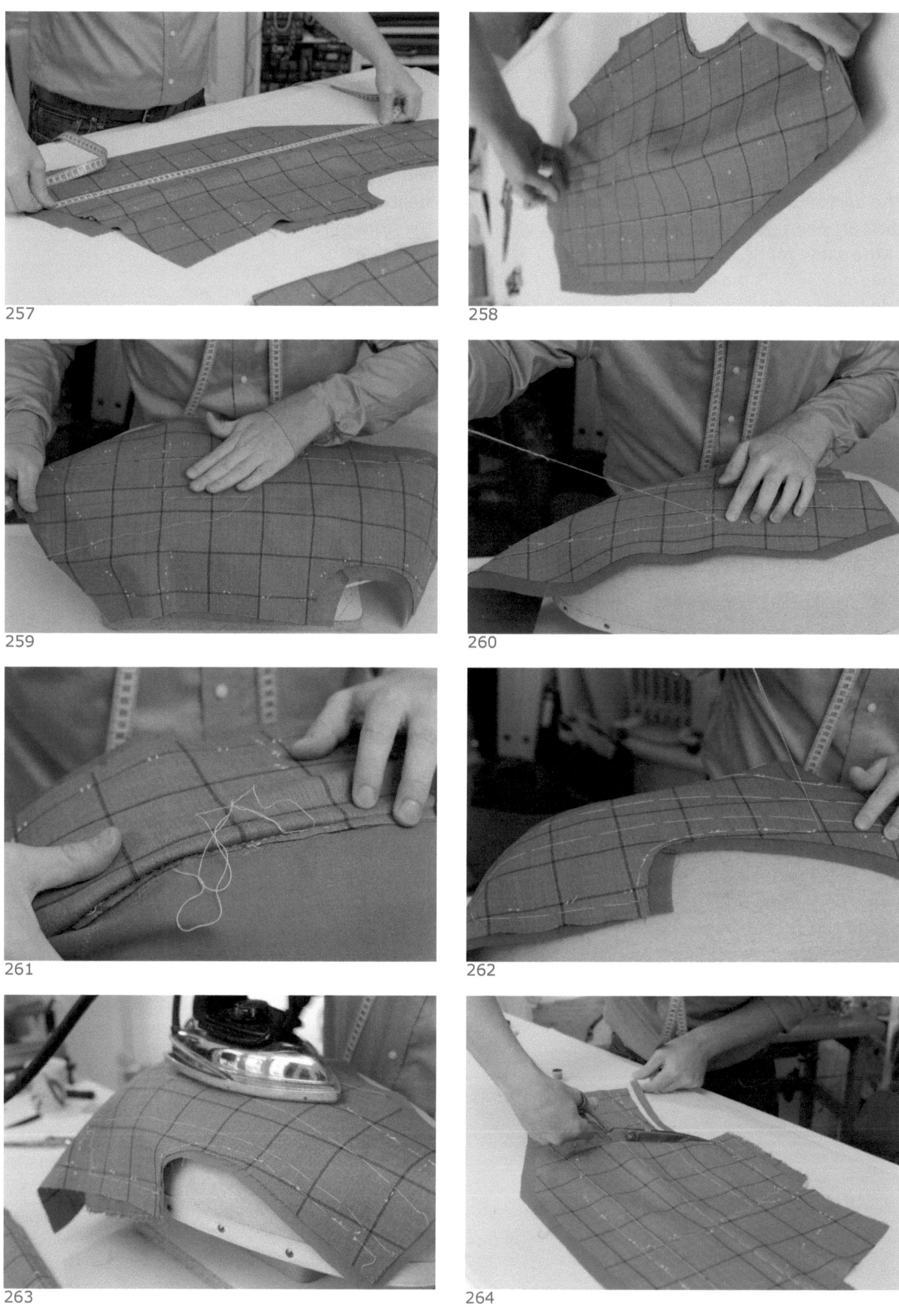

257

258

259

260

261

262

263

264

Basting the front onto the canvas

Picture 257

The front part is placed onto the canvas. The grainline and the fabric pattern should run straight at the front edge. It can be checked with a stretched tape measure or a ruler.

Picture 258

The canvas and fabric are basted together along the fabric pattern to ensure that nothing can shift away. (See drawing, arrow 1)

Picture 259

Now, baste at the waistline from the front edge in the direction of the darts and then upward, along the dart, to the middle of the shoulder. Gently smooth out the fabric, but do not distort the pattern (2).

Picture 260

From the waistline, baste the opening upward (3) and downward the front edge (4). Then, baste down along the dart from the waistline (5).

Attaching the dart

Picture 261

Now, the back front part is folded over at the dart. A loose backstitch can be used to stitch the front part and the canvas together at the seam allowance of the dart. Then, the front part is folded back again.

Picture 262

Now, baste at the waistline to the side seam, upward behind the side seam and along the armhole (6). Ensure the fabric pattern does not warp and the cloth is not basted too loosely or tightly.

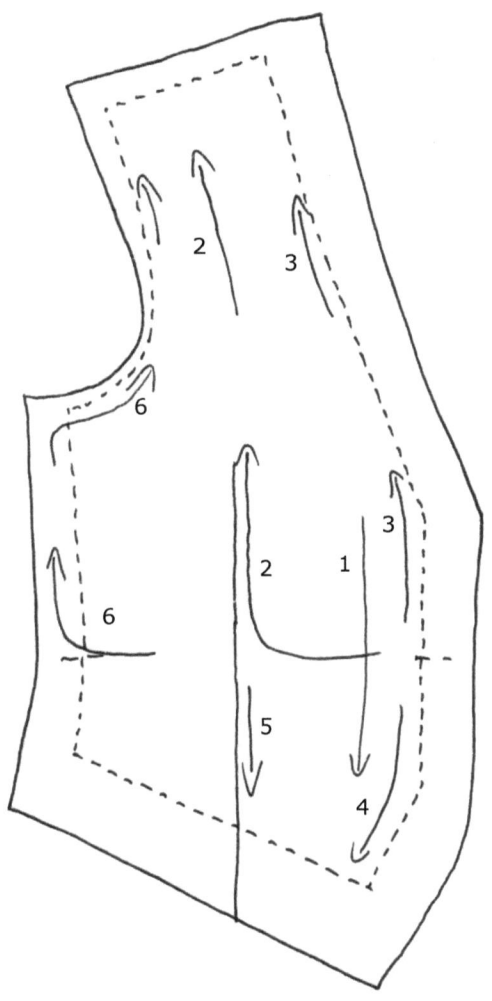

Pressing the front

Picture 263

Now, the front parts are pressed one after the other on the big ironing pad (chest pressing pad).

Picture 264

Finally, the protruding interlining is cut off.

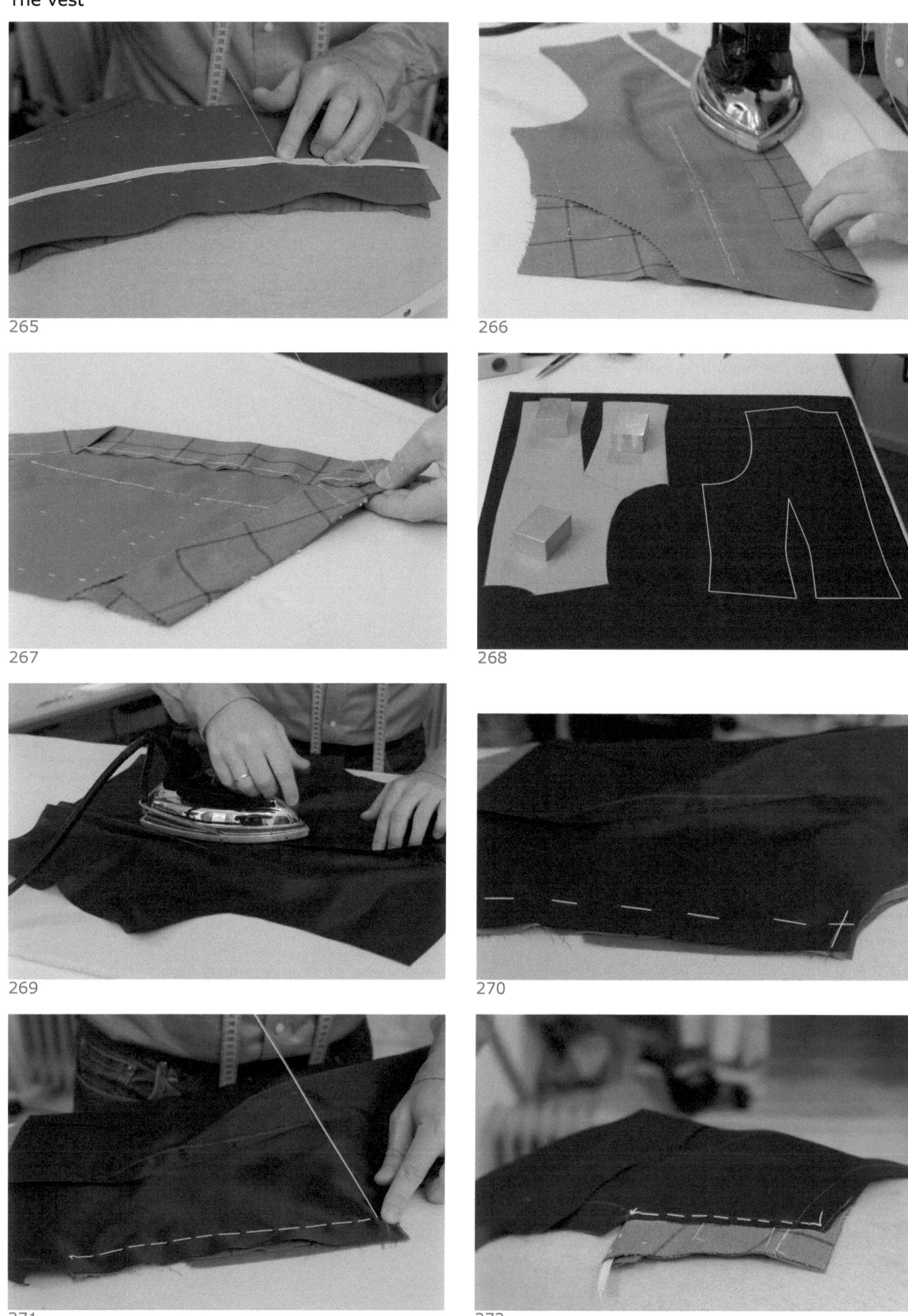

265

266

267

268

269

270

271

272

Securing the opening

Picture 265

A straight linen band (not bias tape) is attached to the opening directly behind the line. It should be kept shorter or longer, depending on the strength of the wearer's chest and the thickness of the outer fabric.

Attaching the band 1 cm shorter is usually sufficient. Of course, fusible tape can also be used.

Picture 266

The front edge, the opening, the length and the lower edge are folded over and ironed flat in this order.

Picture 267

Then, everything can be basted roughly.

Cutting the vest back

Picture 268

Now, the back of the vest is cut. For the first fitting, it is enough to cut it once. The lining in the picture is doubled. So, the back is cut out twice. Then, the dart is transferred to the other back part.

Picture 269

Now, the back seam and the darts are sewn. The back seam is carefully ironed flat, and the darts are ironed towards the side seam.

Take care when ironing lining materials! Once pressed in, wrinkles usually remain visible, even when you try to iron repeatedly.

Picture 270

Now, remark the side seams and the shoulder seams on the lining.

Picture 271

First of all, the side seams of the back are basted to the respective side seams of the front part.

Picture 272

Then, with some fullness, the back lining is basted to the correct shoulder seam on the front.

Vest prepared for the first fitting.

See picture on page 78.

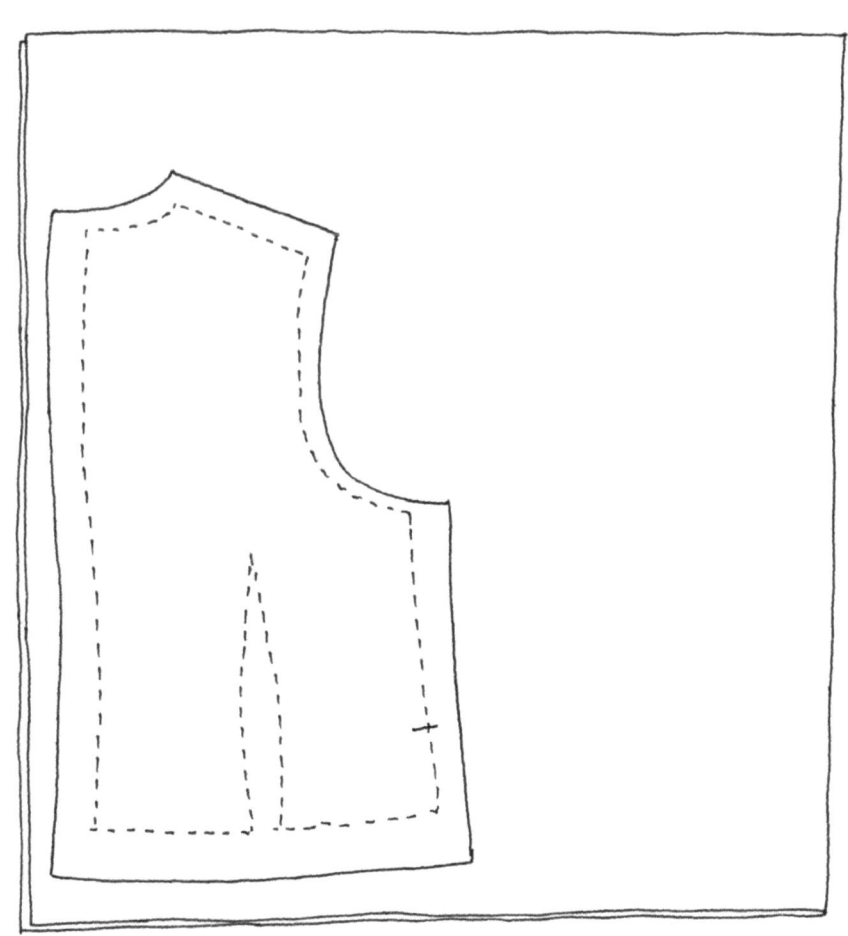

87

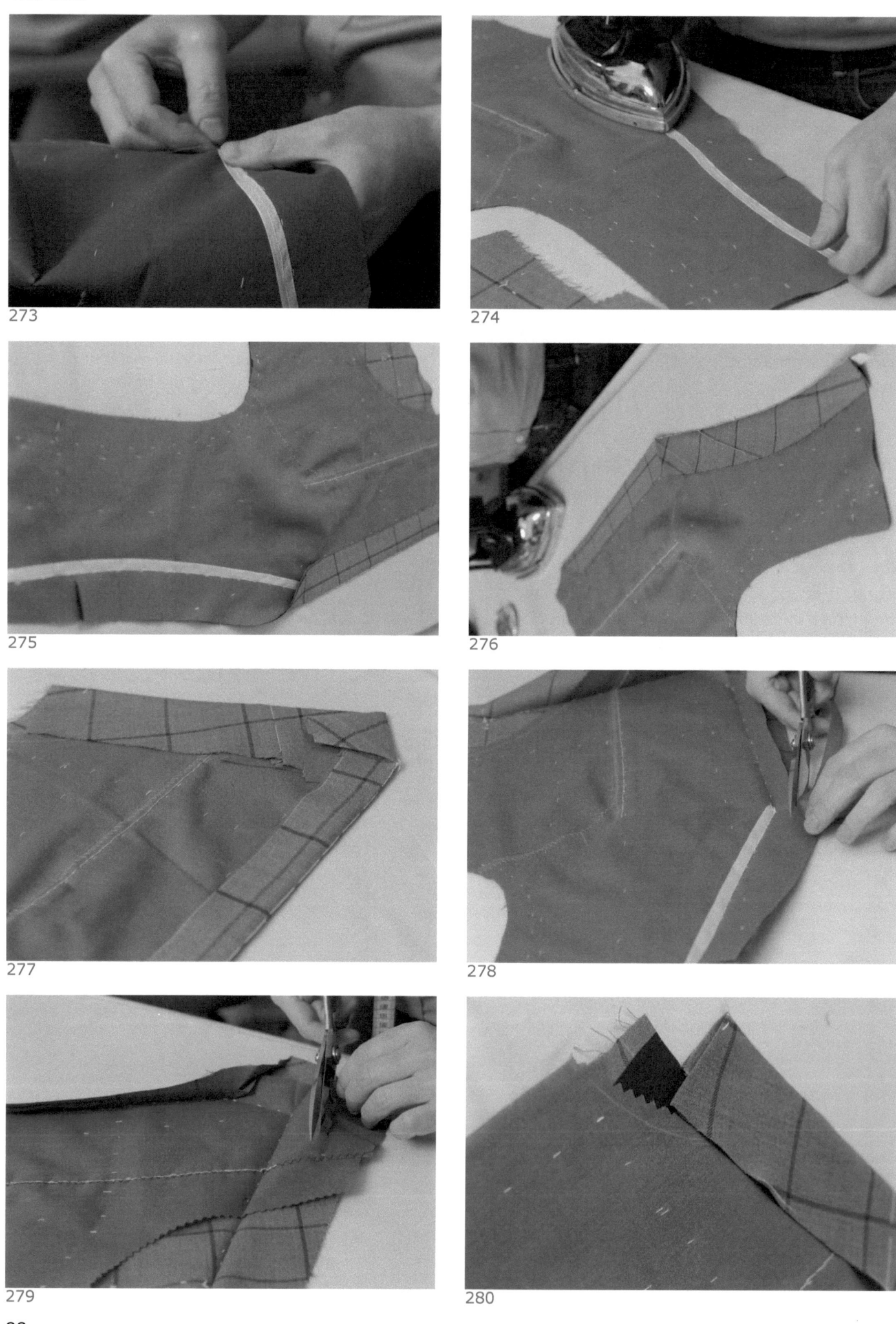

273

274

275

276

277

278

279

280

The vest after the fitting

First, the vest is carefully taken apart.

Preparing the front edge

Then, the front edge and all the alterations are remarked if necessary.

Securing the opening

Picture 273

The position of the linen band may have to be corrected. Consider whether the opening needs to be kept shorter or longer. Then, the linen band is fixed to the canvas with blind stitches. Ensure not to pierce through to the outer fabric.

Picture 274

The opening and the linen tape are now ironed flat. The seam allowance of the canvas is pinched several times so that the facing of the opening can be ironed into shape nicely.

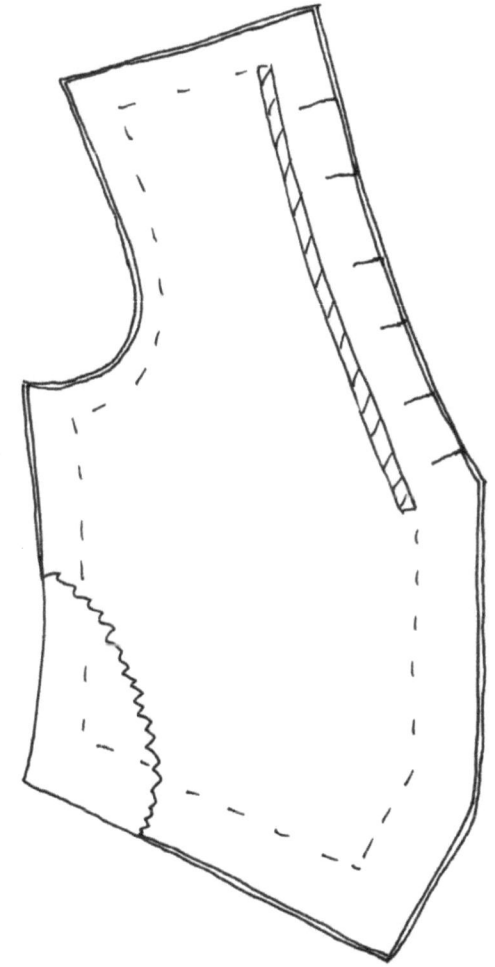

Folding and pressing the edges

Picture 275

Now, the edge is folded over and pressed. You should pay attention to the fabric pattern and its evenness.

Picture 276

Then, the facing is turned over, ironed flat at the opening line, and stretched slightly. So that the opening is nicely curved, the fold at the corner between the front edge and the opening should be at right angles to the front edge.

Picture 277

Now, the hem and the lower front edge are turned over and ironed flat.

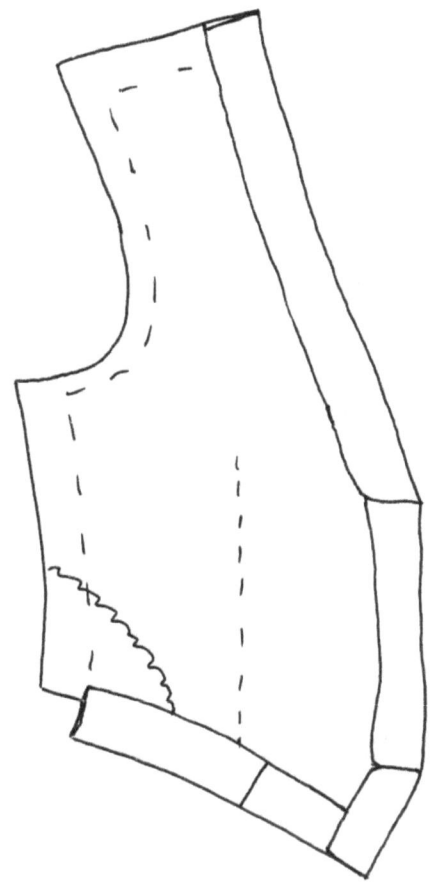

Picture 278

The canvas is cut back to 1 cm at the opening and the front edge.

Picture 279

The canvas is cut back to 2 cm at the lower edge and the hem.

Stabilizing the slit

Picture 280

If the vest has a slit at the side seam, a very thin fusible interlining is pressed on at this area. Then, the seam allowance is pinched, turned over and ironed flat.

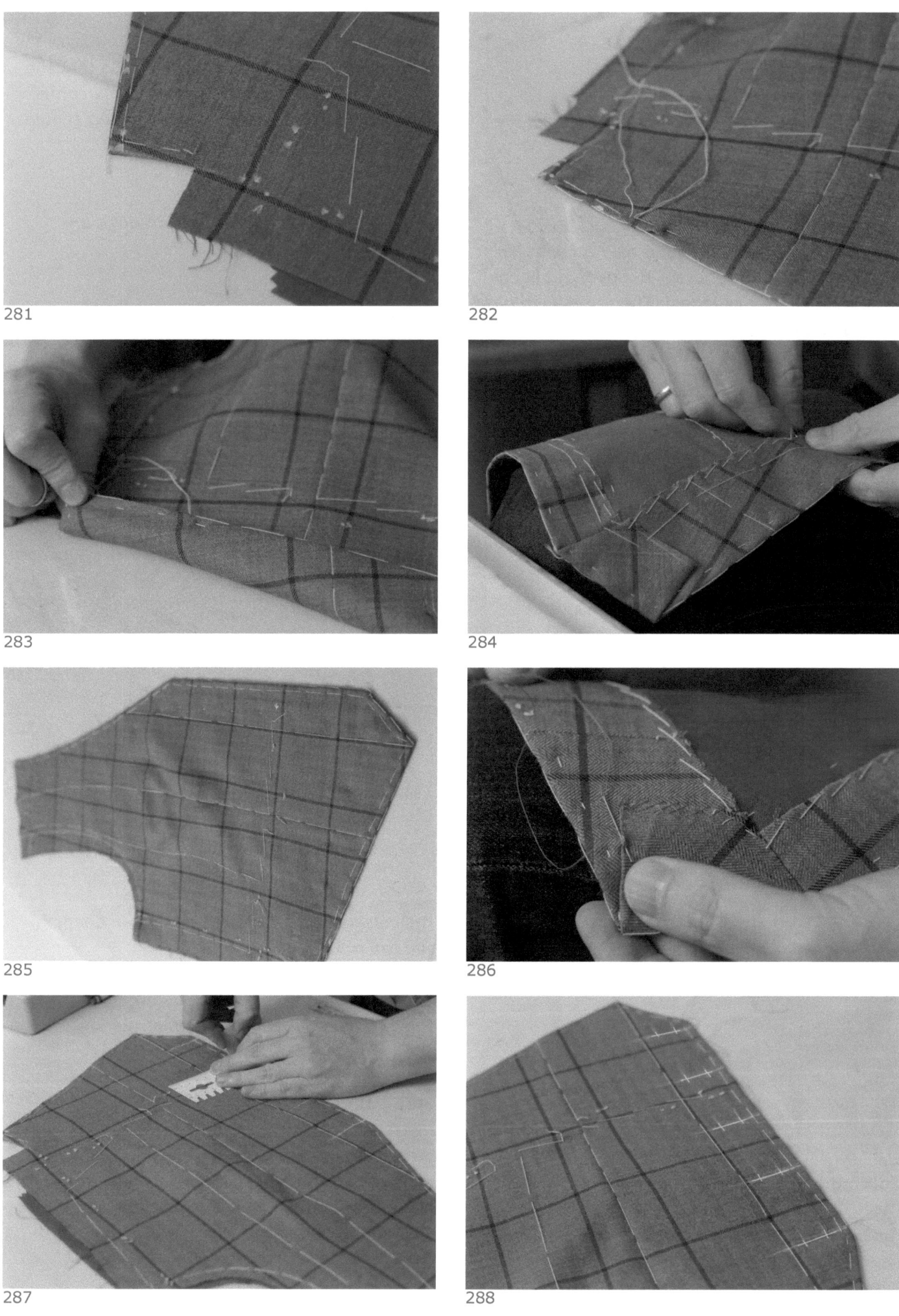

281

282

283

284

285

286

287

288

Pictures 281/282/283
The slit, the lower edge, the front edge and the opening are basted into place.

Attaching the facing

Pictures 284/285
The facing is fixed to the canvas with a pad-stitch. Ensure it is only attached to the canvas. All ironed-in folds at the facing are now closed with a blind stitch.

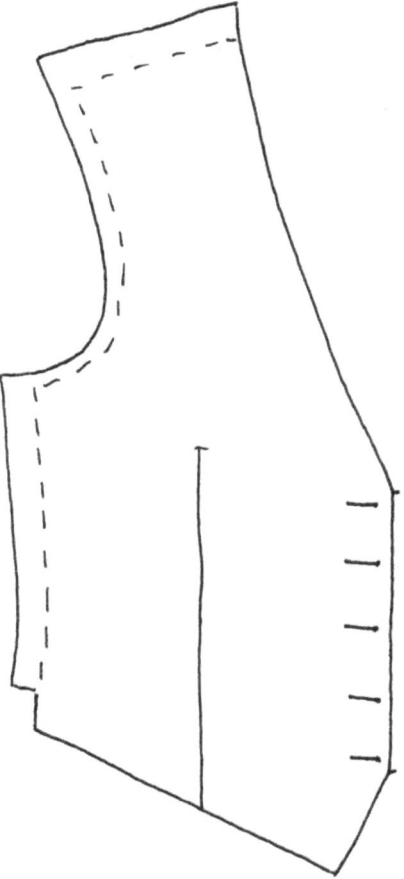

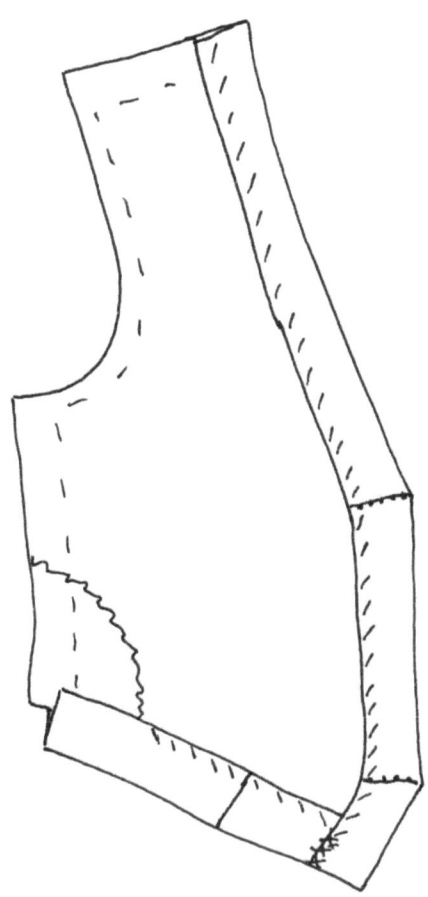

Picture 288
Then, the buttonholes are stitched all around with a small stitch using the sewing machine. It is a safeguard so that the buttonhole does not fray when knotted.

Securing the lower edge

Picture 286
The hem allowance at the lower end is secured with cross-stitches, and the rest is closed with blind stitches.

Marking the buttonholes

Picture 287
Now, mark the buttonholes on the front edge of the left front piece.
You should always choose an uneven number of buttonholes. It just looks better. According to your design, the distance can be between 5.5 and 7 cm.

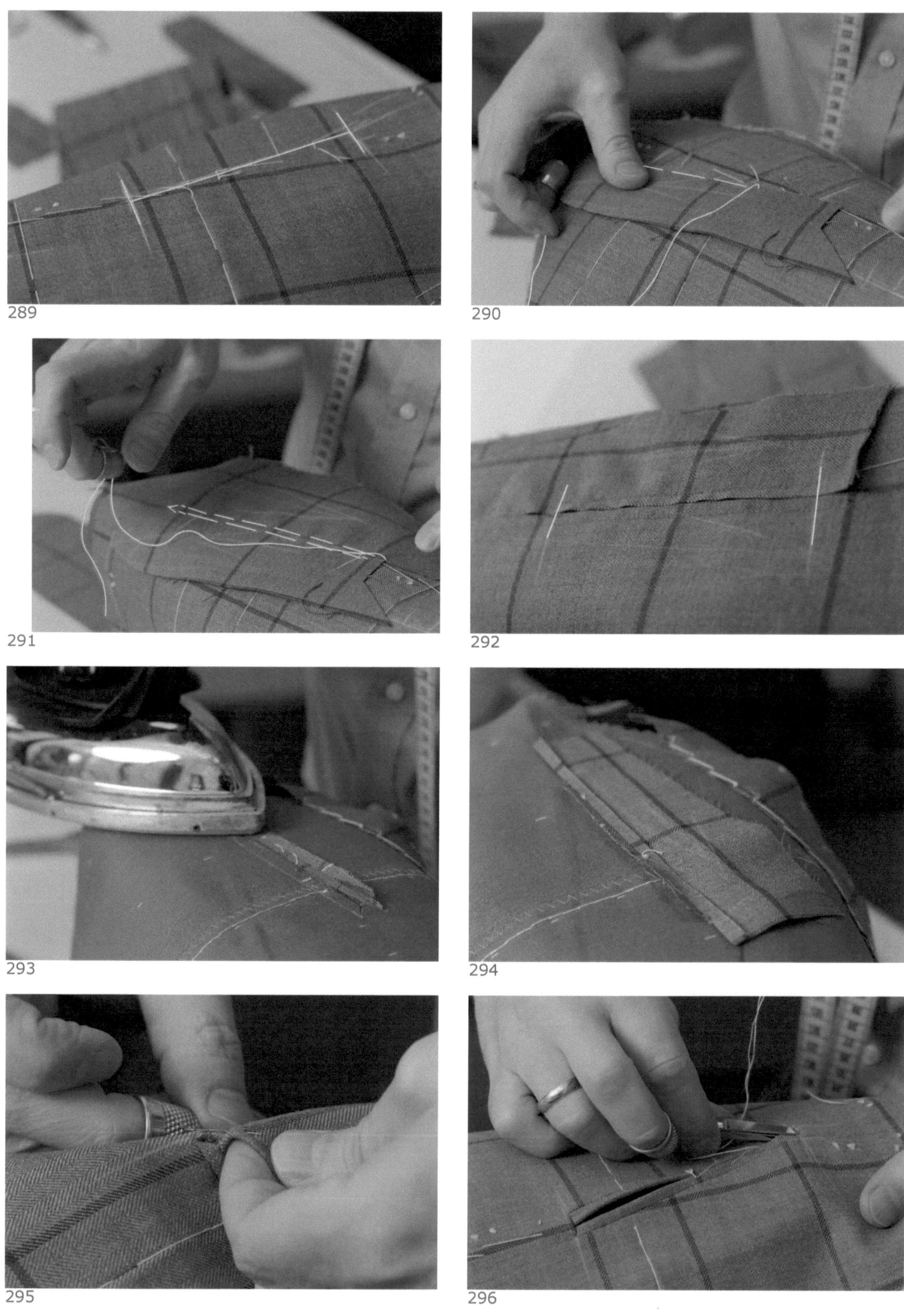

289

290

291

292

293

294

295

296

Remarking the pockets

Picture 289

Both front pieces must be marked in exactly the same position. You can orient yourself on a fabric pattern; otherwise, you have to measure precisely.

Pictures 290/291

Then, the jets are attached one after the other (note the pile), and the marks for the pocket's beginning and end are transferred up onto the jets. If the lower jet is wide enough, it can be used as a part of the pocket bag.

Picture 292

The jets are sewn by approximately 0.5 cm. The stitching's beginning and end must meet the marking exactly; otherwise, the pocket will look crooked.

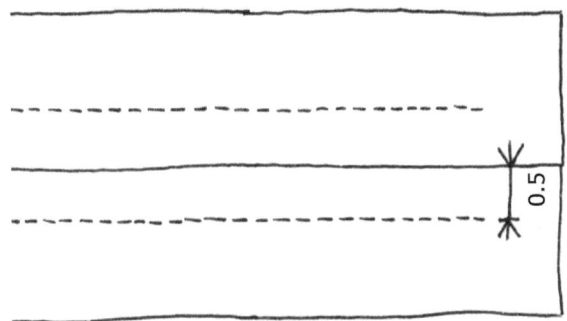

Cut open the pocket opening

Picture 293

After checking the evenness of the seams and the locked ends, the pocket opening can be carefully cut open. The incisions at the end are made in a triangle shape and should be as close to the seam as possible, just before the end of the last stitch.

Attention: the seam allowances of the jets are pushed to the side and not cut!

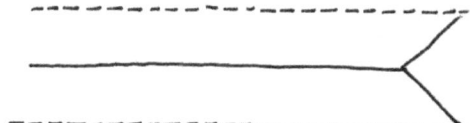

Ironing flat the jets

The vest is now held at the bottom, so the lower jet hangs down.

Then, the vest is carefully pulled over the ironing pad. This action flips the lower jet, enabling the seam allowance to be pressed open. It is important to proceed with caution, particularly at the corner, as it will make it easier to sew the jet by hand later.

Picture 294

The upper jet is pulled through the pocket opening, and the seam is carefully ironed flat. Be careful, by pulling out the upper jet; the lower jet can slip easily!

Handsewing the jets

Picture 295

After everything has been adequately ironed flat, the jets can be formed. The seam allowance of the jet disappears into the fabric of the jet strip.

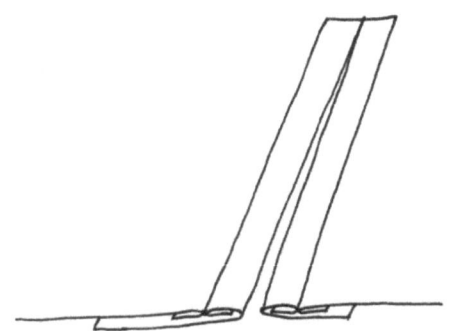

Then, the jet is hand-sewn with a quick sinking stitch precisely in the seam shadow. The jet width is formed with the left hand and should, of course, be absolutely even, each for itself and both with each other. The width is approximately 0.5 cm. More usually looks chunky and less too filigree.

Pushing through the triangles

Picture 296

The triangles are now carefully pushed inwards (see picture 99 on page 42).

The vest

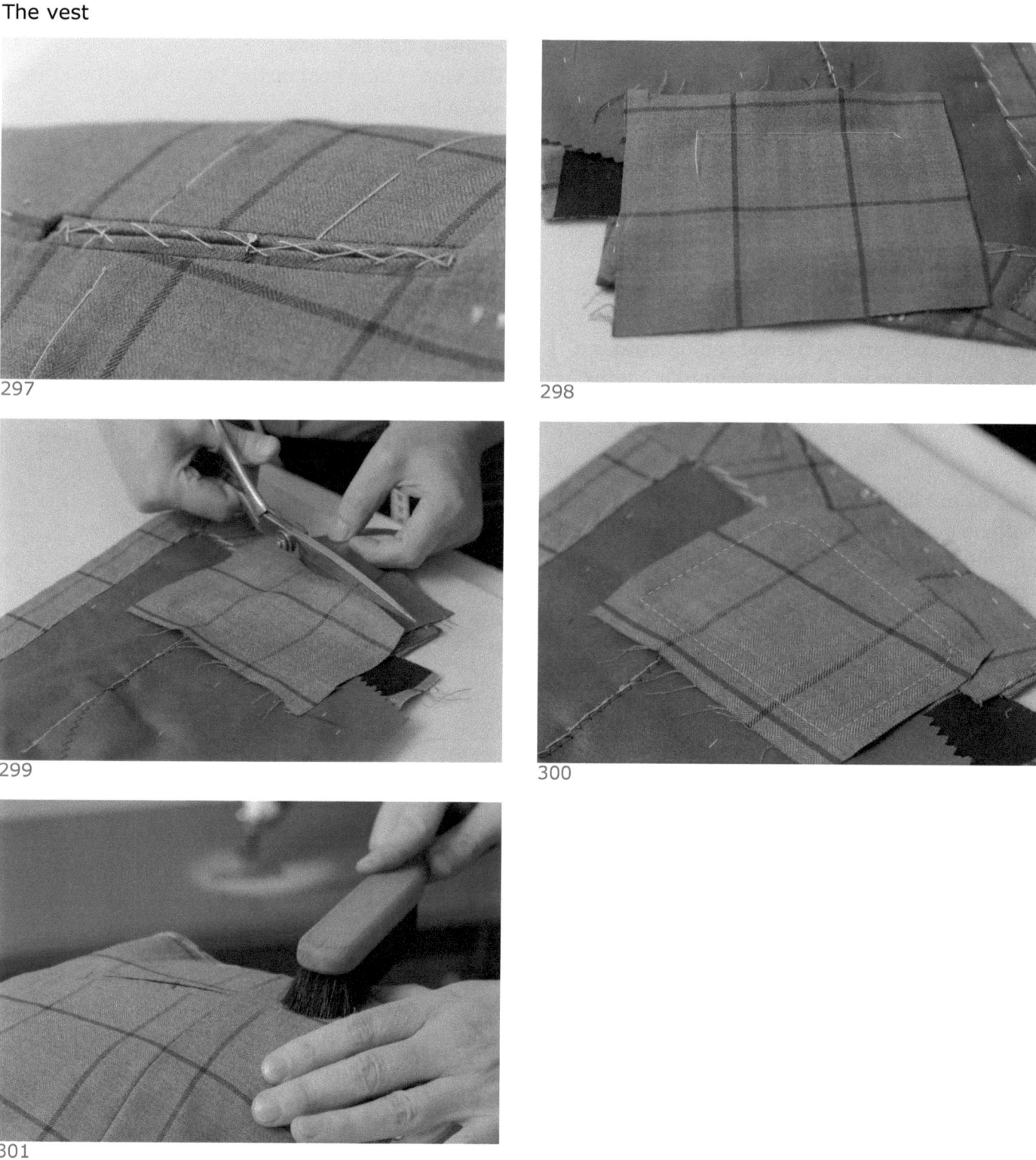

297

298

299

300

301

Basting the pocket opening together

Picture 297
The jets are now basted together. A fabric pattern must be considered.

Then, the corners can be secured with the sewing machine. Particular care should be taken here, as otherwise, the corners might fray later. The sewing machine needle is inserted precisely in the corner; then it is sewn to the other corner, back and forward again (see also page 56, picture 156).

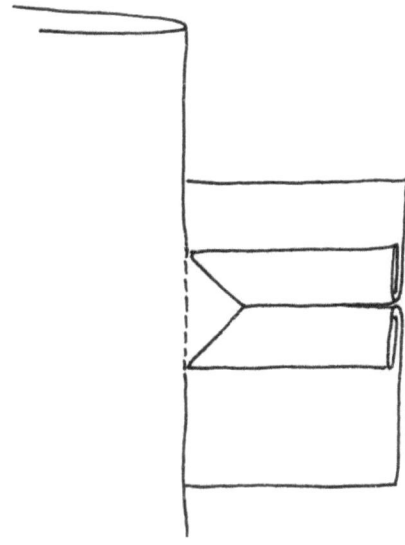

Now, the lower jet can be secured from the back, making it more durable. Turn the lower jet to the right and the rest of the vest to the left. Only the previously hand-sewn jet strip is fixed into place. The outer fabric remains completely untouched.

Attaching the facing

Picture 298
The pocket facing is attached with a basting stitch. A fabric pattern should be the same for both pockets.

Picture 299
The pocket facing is cut away by approximately 2.5 cm above the hem.

Picture 300
Now, the pocket bag is closed all around, what also secures the upper jet.

Grading down the jets

Then, the jets are graded down at the ends. Two of the three layers are cut away. What means, that the seam allowances are less able to bulge through the outer fabric.

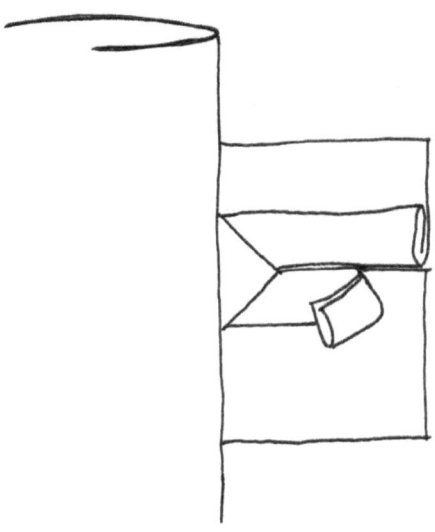

Brushing off the chalk

Picture 301
Finally, the chalk is brushed off and the pocket is closed with a basting stitch, right in the seam shadow of the lower jet.

Video instructions for jetted pockets

To make jetted pockets, follow the video 'jetted pocket with flap' in the jacket videos section.

Link to the
jacket videos

https://www.becomeatailor.com/videos-jacket

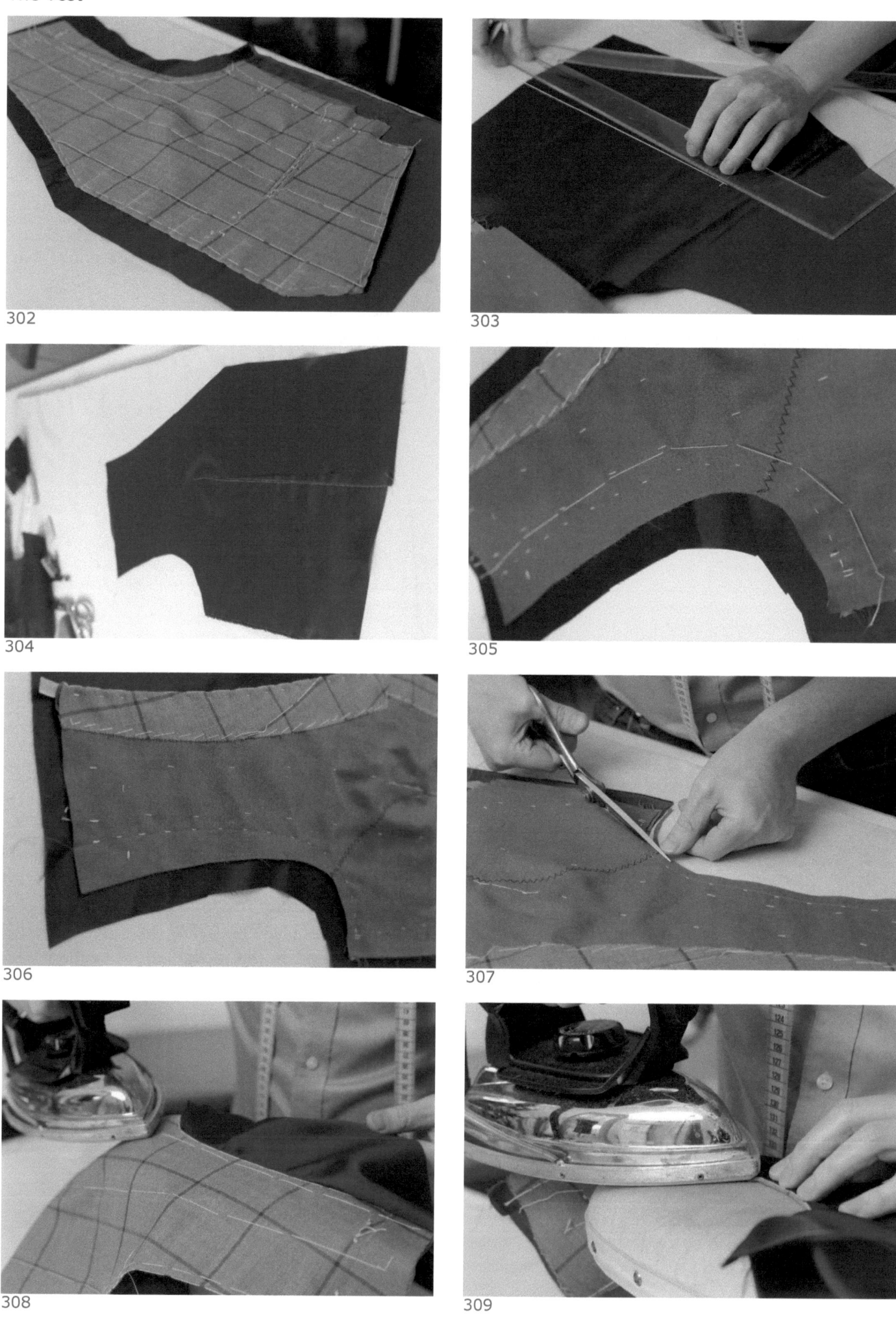

302

303

304

305

306

307

308

309

Cutting the front lining

Picture 302

The front part is placed on a piece of lining; then the lining is cut out generously. Then, the position of the dart is marked.

Re-marking the dart

Picture 303

Now, the dart is transferred to the other front lining.

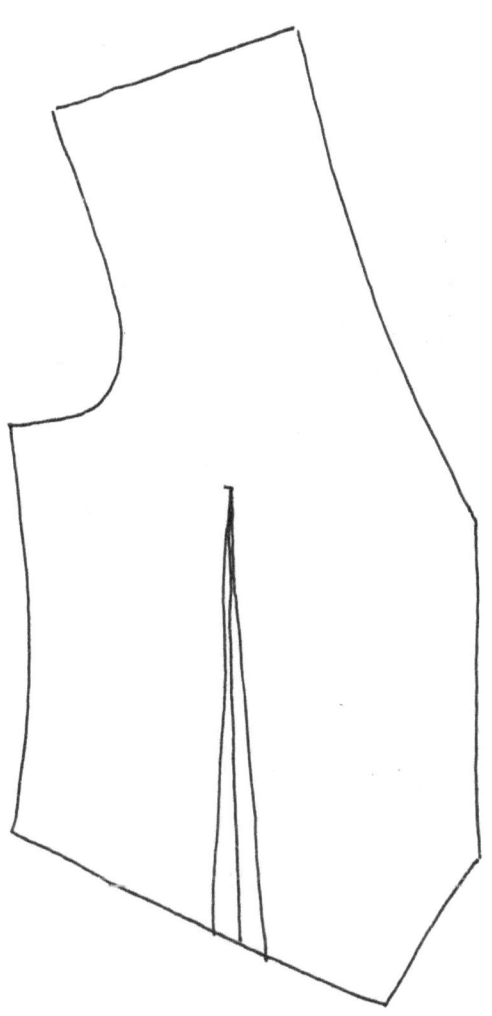

Sewing the darts

Picture 304

Then, the darts are sewn and ironed over from the left side towards the front edge.

Sewing the front armhole

Picture 305

Now, the front part and the lining are placed right sides together. The darts must be in the same position. Then, both pieces are connected at the armhole with basting stitches or pins.

Picture 306

The armhole is sewn at the outer side of the armhole marking, right beside the basting stitches.

Pressing the armhole

Picture 307

Then, the seam allowance is cut off evenly. If necessary, it can be pinched so it does not tens in the curve.

Picture 308

The lining is folded back and ironed flat at the armhole on the shoulder ironing pad.

Picture 309

Then, the armhole is ironed over so that approximately 2 mm of the outer fabric is visible on the inside; this leaves enough space to sink-stitch the edge of the armhole.
All basting threads at the armhole can now be removed.

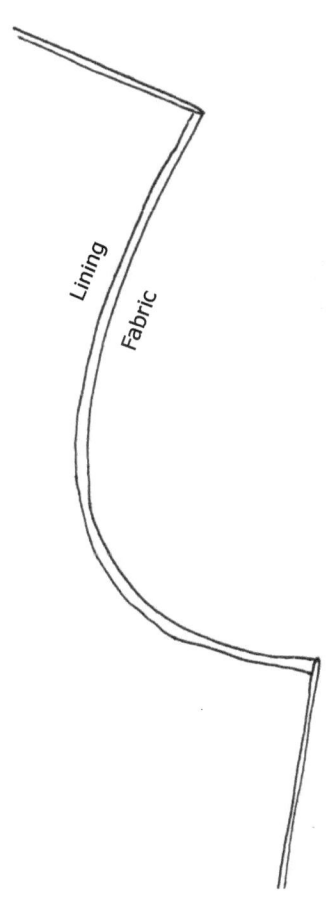

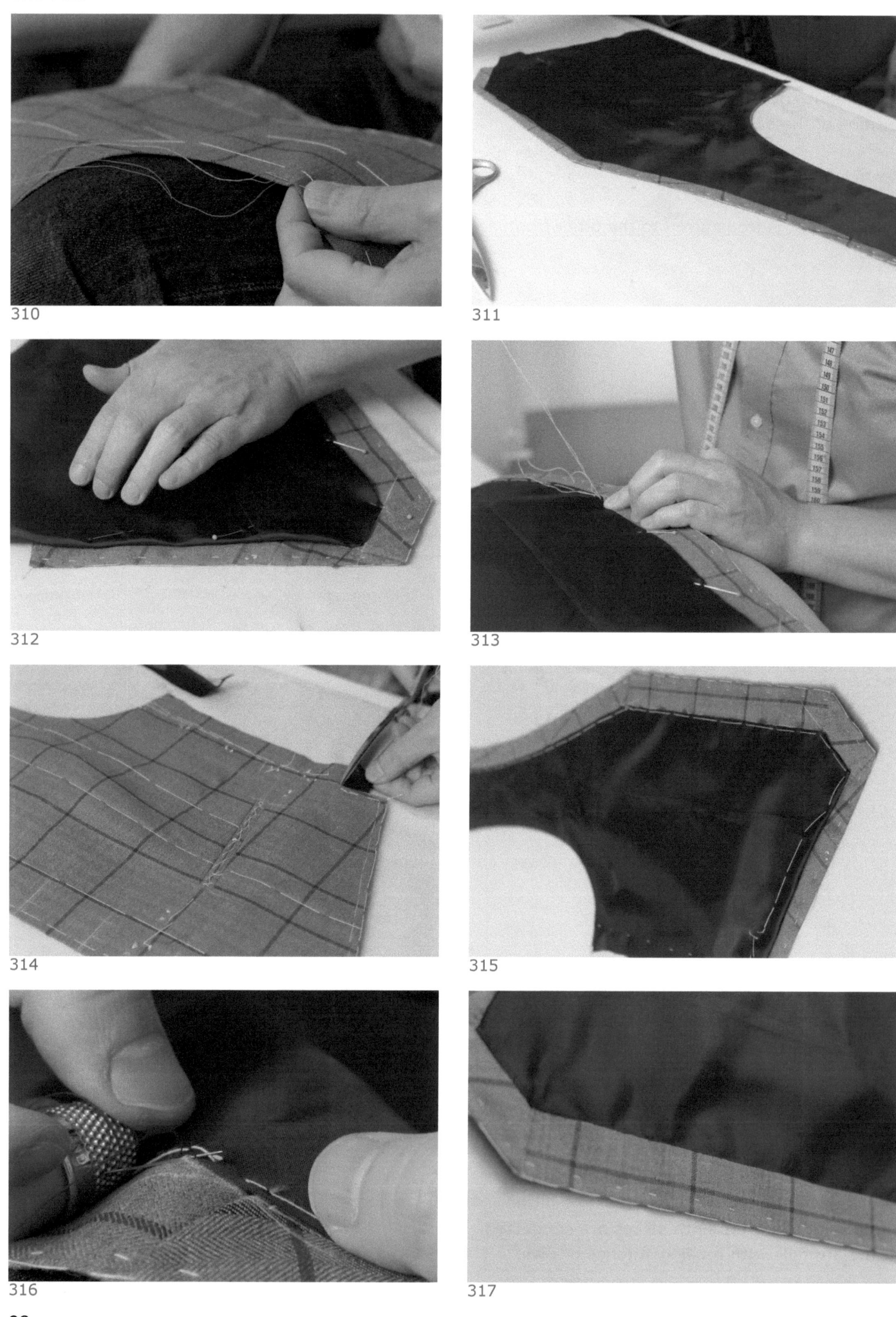

310

311

312

313

314

315

316

317

Sink-stitching the armhole

Picture 310

Now, the edge of the armhole is sewn by hand with a quick sinking stitch (see page 11).
Then, the lining line is drawn in with chalk on the facing at the opening and the front edge, as well as at the lower edge; this should run about 3.5 to 4 cm away from the edge.

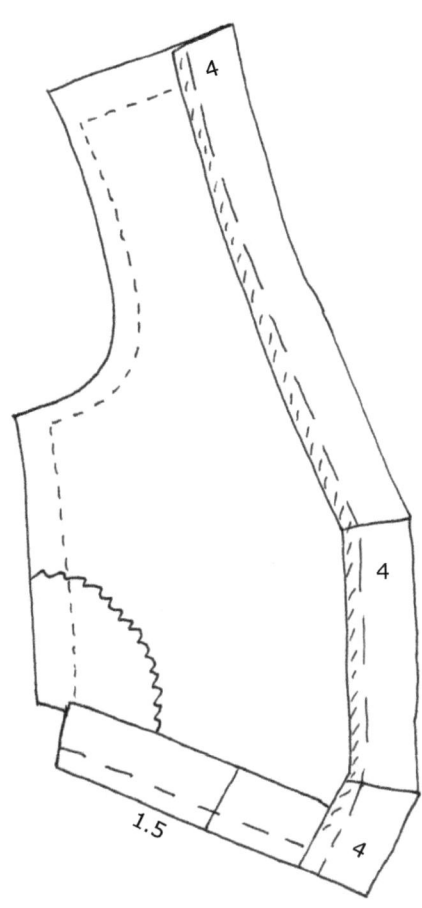

Picture 311

The darts of the lining and the front part are placed on top of one another and pinned or basted. The lining can be cut back a little.

Attaching and blind stitching the lining

Picture 312

Then, the lining is pinned to the marked calk line with a bit of extra width (approximately 5 mm).
At the hem, the lining should run approximately 1.5 cm from the edge. An expansion fold is integrated here.

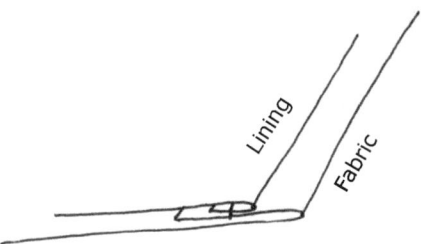

Picture 313

Then, the lining is basted, ensuring a straight and even course.

Picture 314

If the vest has slits at the side seams, the lining is pinched at the proper place.

Picture 315

The left and right front pieces should also look the same at the lining inside the vest.
Now the lining is folded inwards at the slit and basted.
At the side seam, the lining is basted down from the top just behind the seam.

Pictures 316/317

Finally, the lining is carefully and evenly blind-stitched. The stitches should, of course, not be visible on the right side of the fabric.

318

319

320

321

322

323

324

325

Sewing the back lining

Picture 318

The first back lining that was used at the fitting is now re-marked.

Then, the second is cut in the same way, and the back seam and darts are sewn. Now, both lining parts are placed with the right sides together. To secure them, fix all seams with pins, ensuring that the position of the darts corresponds. The length of the shoulder and side seams must match the front part; here, the lining should also have a little extra width (approximately 5 mm).

Belt

If you want, you can fix a belt on the back of the vest at the waistline level.

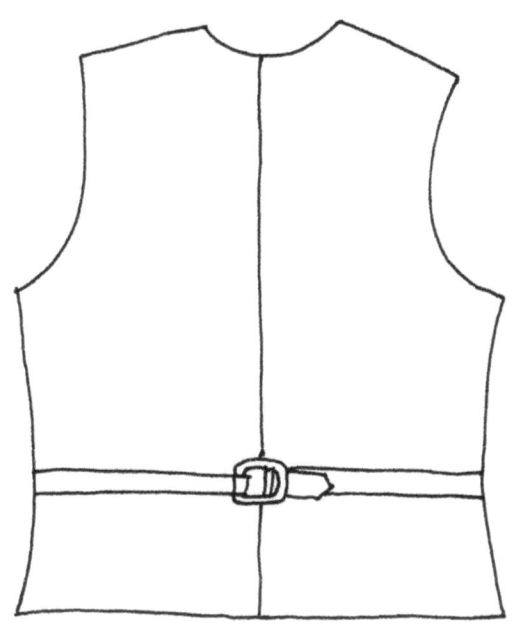

Hem at the center back

The hem at the back seam can be sewn with a v-shape vent.

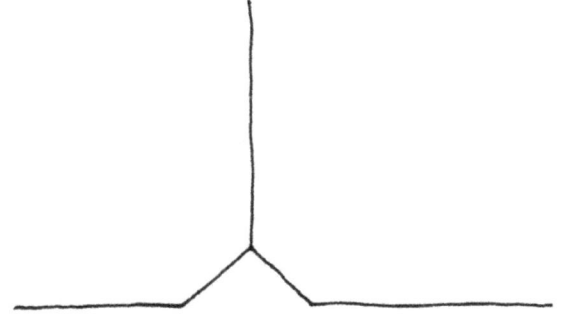

Securing the neckline

Picture 319

When sewing the neckline, a straight piece of lining is placed underneath at the center back. It reinforces the back seam and prevents it from tearing at the neck. Now, the armhole and the hem are sewn.

The seam allowances at the neck and armholes are cut back to approximately 1 cm and not pinched. About 4 cm seam allowance can be left at the hem.

Picture 320

First, the seam allowance is folded to one side and ironed flat.

Picture 321

After that, the entire edge can be ironed flat more easily.

Picture 322

The course of the seam at the side and shoulder seam are marked with sublimating chalk. Regular tailoring chalk is very difficult to remove from the lining.

Blindstitching the back

Pictures 323/324

Now, the side seam of the back is placed onto the side seam of the front part and pinned with needles. The course should be even, and there should be extra length (approximately 5 mm) in the lining.

Picture 325

Then, the same is done at the inner side seam.

326

327

328

329

330

331

332

333

Basting the back lining

Picture 326

The back lining is now basted at the side and the shoulder seams.

Picture 327

Then, the lining is blind-stitched outside and inside with an even course and stitch.
A small bar at the slit can prevent it from tearing.

Sink-stitching the edges

Pictures 328

The hem, the lower front edge, the front edge and the opening are sewn by hand with a quick sink stitch. Even with the faster sewing option, you can work carefully so that the stitch is barely visible on the inside.

Pictures 329/330

The carefully sewn variant of the sinking stitch takes much longer, and the difference is hardly noticeable. (See also hand stitches on page 11)

Sewing the buttonholes

Picture 331

Now, "the eyes" for the buttonholes are punched in with the punch pliers. When punching, a piece of leather should be placed underneath; this will extend the life of the pliers.
The distance between the hole and the front edge should be approximately 1.5 cm and be the same for all holes. The distance between the buttonholes should also be checked repeatedly before punching.

Picture 332

Then, the buttonholes are carefully and evenly cut open with a length of approximately 1.7 cm (including the hole). To determine the size of the buttonholes, add 2 mm to the diameter of the button.

Picture 333

Now, the buttonholes are carefully knotted (see page 51).

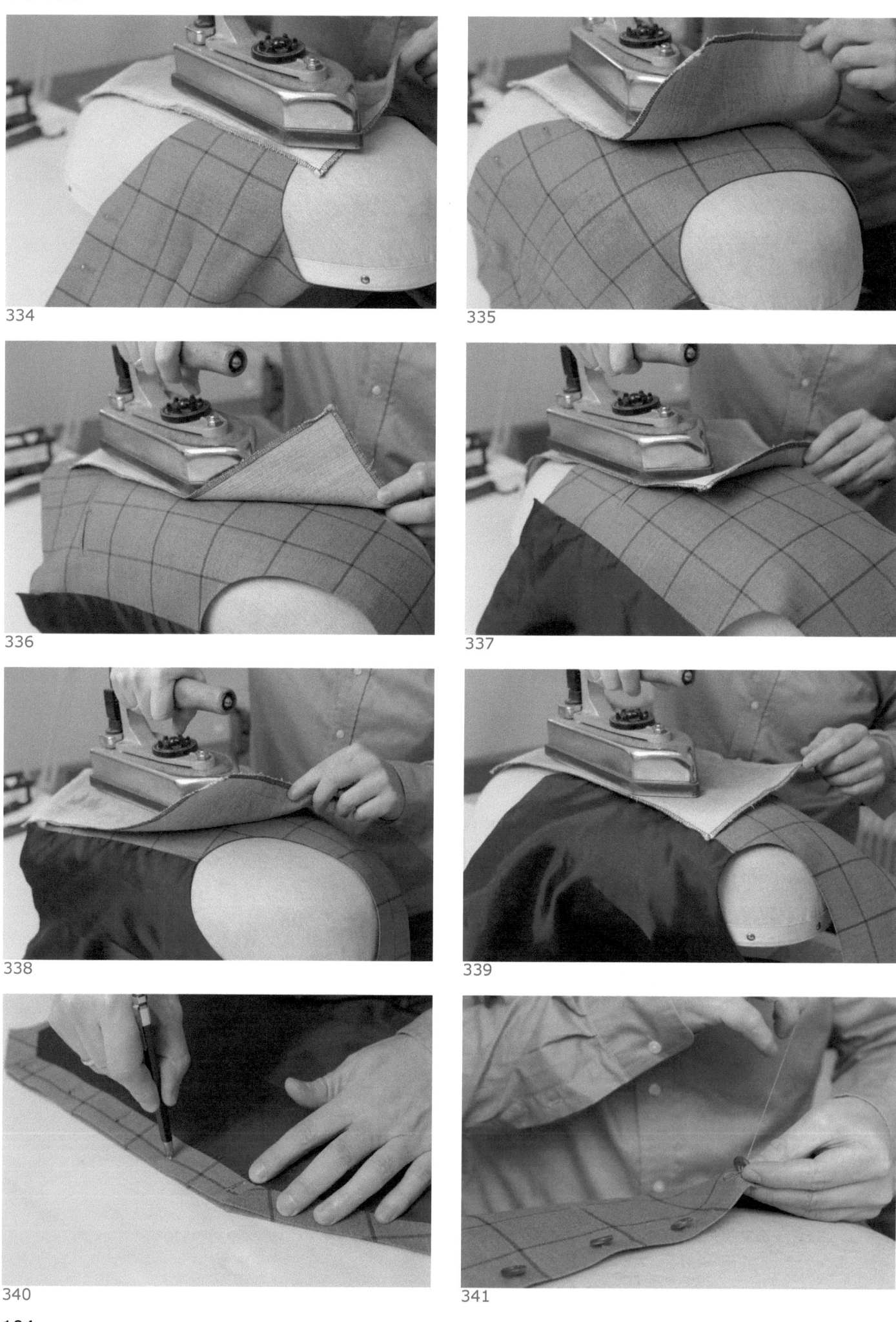

334

335

336

337

338

339

340

341

Pressing the vest

The vest is pressed part by part on the torso pressing pad with an ironing cloth and a heavy iron. The ironing cloth is moistened with a fabric brush or a spray bottle and ironed dry. The resulting steam and the pressure of the heavy iron ensure a smooth front part. The vest is always placed on the ironing pad in such a way that the natural shape is supported.

Picture 334

To begin, carefully press the shoulder seam and the upper part of the armhole.

Picture 335

Next, move on to the opening and the lower part of the armhole.

Picture 336

The front edge with the buttonholes should be pressed next,

Picture 337

followed by the pocket and lower edge.

Picture 338

Then, carefully press the dart,

Picture 339

...

and then move on to the side seam. Finally, the inner and back linings should be ironed with a remnant piece of the lining as an ironing cloth, applying light pressure without moisture for the best results.

Let the vest cool down

Letting the vest cool down on the dress form after ironing is important to avoid any creases. This will ensure the vest retains its shape and looks neat when worn.

Marking the buttons

Picture 340

The front parts are placed together on the right sides. Once they're aligned, you can mark the position of the buttons using a chalk pen or pins.

Attaching the buttons

Picture 341

As the final, significant steps, the buttons are sewn on with waxed buttonhole silk and a short stem. The buttonhole silk is pulled over a beeswax candle, then placed between a folded piece of blotting paper, and ironed off. It ensures that not too much wax gets stuck on the yarn. When sewing, the yarn "sticks together", and the button cannot come off quickly. The vest should be treated as carefully as possible and lie flat so it does not have to be ironed again.

Be careful when working with beeswax! It is almost impossible to remove from lining and silk.

The slanted pockets

342

The fly with a zipper

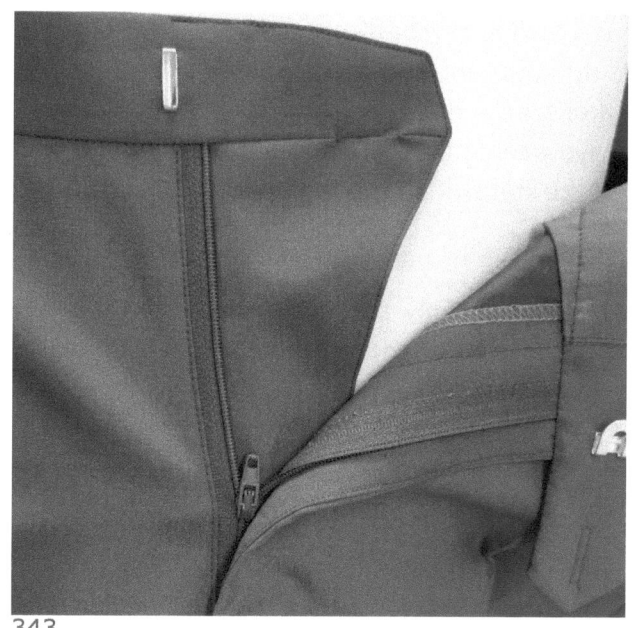

343

The turnup

344

The welted pockets

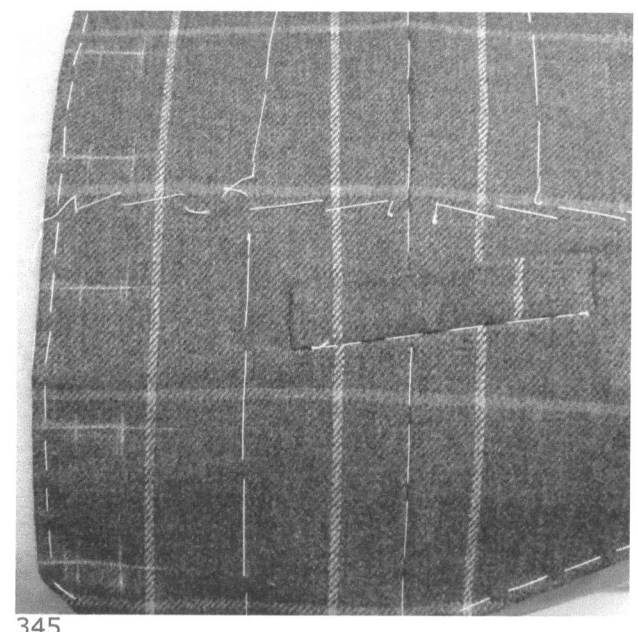

345

Link to the
trousers videos

https://www.becomeatailor.com/videos-trousers/

Link to the
vest videos

https://www.becomeatailor.com/videos-waistcoat/

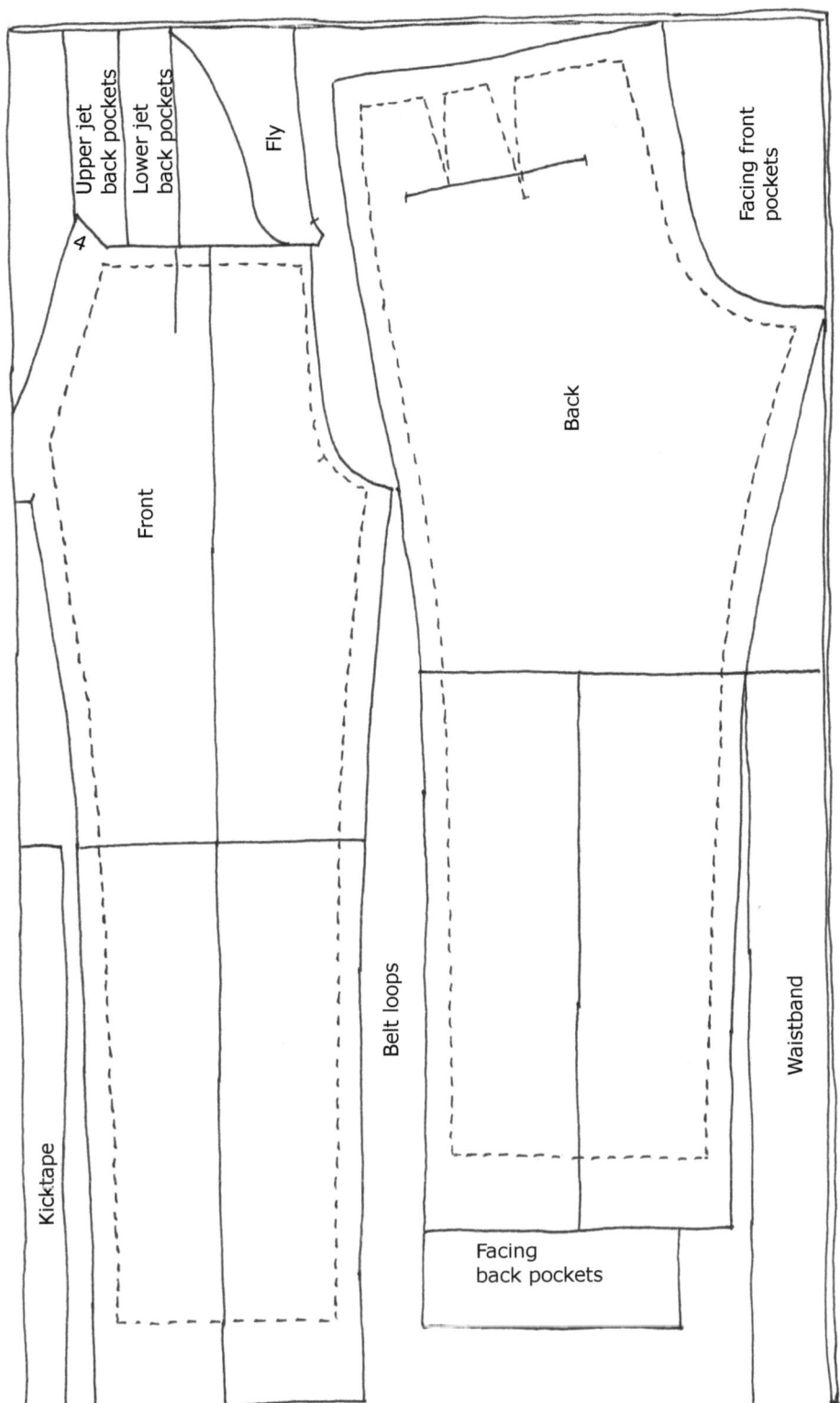

Upper jet back pockets

Lower jet back pockets

Fly

Facing front pockets

Back

Front

Belt loops

Waistband

Kicktape

Facing back pockets

Cutting pants with slanted pockets

If the front trousers get slanted pockets, this must be included in the cutting process. You can simply cut away the fabric at the opening and sew on a facing, but this variation is neater and more excellent. When cutting, you must pay attention to the pile and grainline. (See p. 33)

Measurements for the waistband lining and the pocket bags

Back pocket bag: Length 45 cm, width 20 cm
Waistband lining:
Length 1/2 *WB* + 10 cm, width 11.5 cm
Lining for the fly extension:
Length 30 cm, width 15 cm
The pocket bag of the slanted pockets is cut like that of the jetted pockets (See pic. 139 on p. 52). For the waistband horsehair, see p. 33.

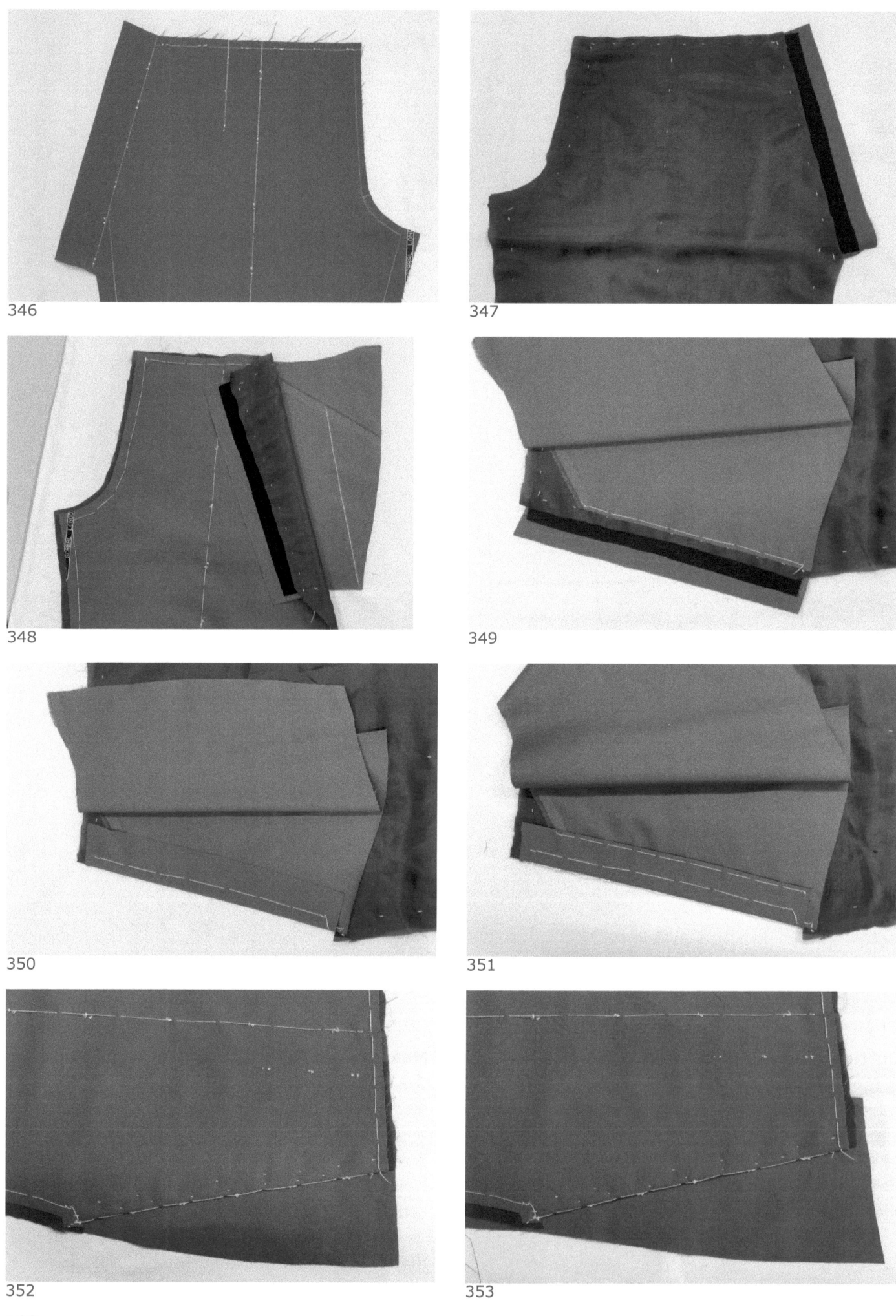

346

347

348

349

350

351

352

353

Tailor tacking the front with slanted pockets

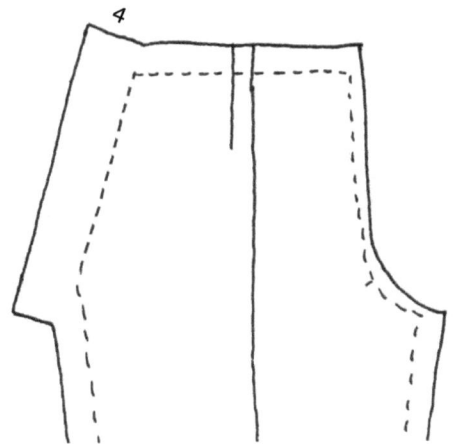

Picture 346

At the front trousers, stitches are tucked in at the waistline, in the front trousers break, at the pleat and the pocket opening.

The edge of the slanted pocket is secured on the wrong side of the fabric with a straight fusible band or a straight piece of lining to prevent it from expanding.

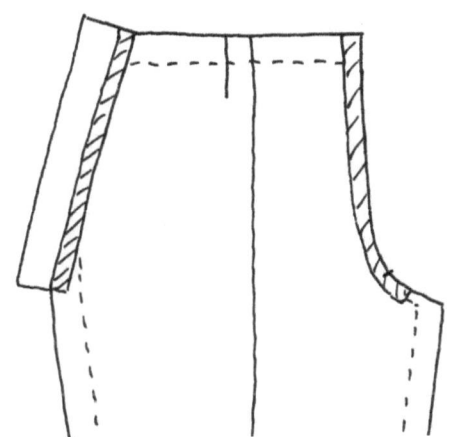

Picture 347

The front lining has been basted, but the edges on the front are only finished after the pocket has been completed (see page 36).

Placing the pocket bag

Picture 348

The pocket bag is cut as on page 52 (Pictures 139/140). Then, it is placed under the front trousers into the correct position. At the lower end, it should be approximately 1 cm too long at the side seam and extend at least to the top edge of the waistline. The slope of the pocket opening is transferred to the pocket bag. The bias cut side of the pocket bag is facing upward. Nothing should slip in this process.

At the mark, the pocket bag is cut back at the top part only.

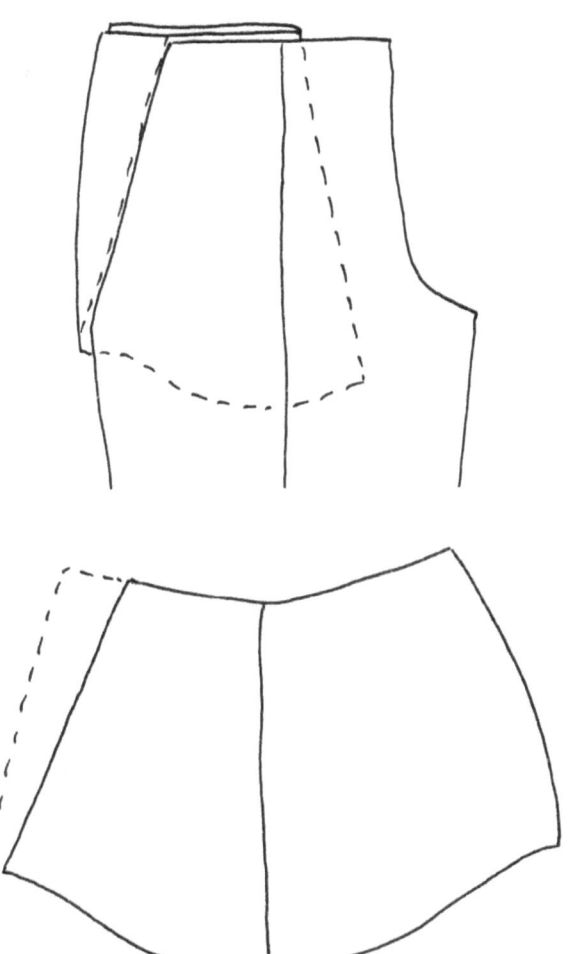

Picture 349

Now, the cut-back edge of the pocket bag is placed directly at the edge of the pocket opening and basted.

Picture 350

Then, the facing (seam allowance) is folded over and ironed flat. The facing, the pocket bag, and the front trousers are basted together.

Picture 351

Either the edge of the facing has been serged with the overlock sewing machine, or it is now turned in and pinned to the pocket bag. A piece of cardboard can be placed between the pocket bag and the front lining.

The pocket facing

Pictures 352/353

The pocket facing is placed on the other side of the pocket bag. The grainline and fabric pattern have to fit the front trousers.

354

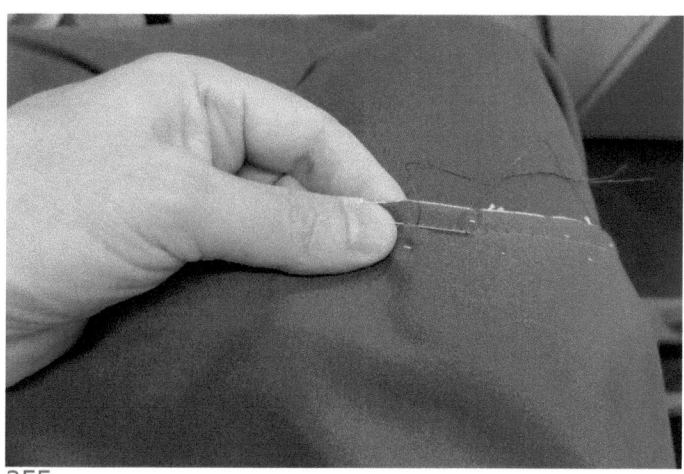

355

356

357

358

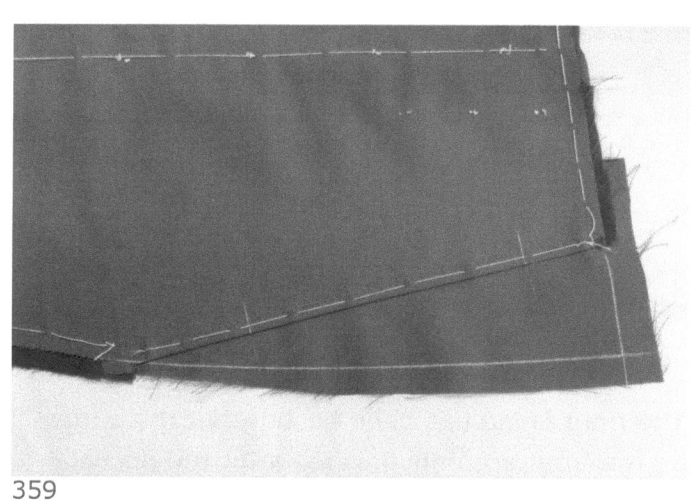

359

360

The pocket facing

Picture 354

Now, the pocket facing is basted without slipping. Then, it has to be cut back by approximately 0.75 cm at the lower edge so the seam does not become too thick later.

Picture 355

Now, the pocket opening's edge can either be sewn by hand with a prick stitch or sewn with a sewing machine by a width of approximately 0.75 cm.

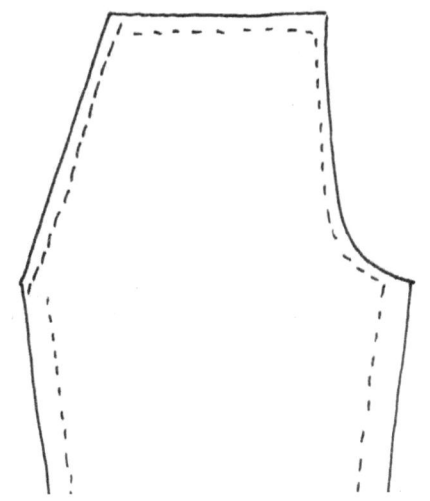

Picture 356

Sewing the facing

The facing and the folded-over facing of the pocket opening are then sewn onto the front trousers.

Closing the pocket bag

Bild 357

Then, the pocket bag is placed with the right sides facing each other and closed from the fold at the lower seam. Now, it is turned outside in, and the front tip is beautifully worked out with the awl or bone folder.
The seam can be pressed down with your fingers.

Picture 358

The facing and all seam allowances inside the bag should now be laid neatly and smoothly. Then, the lower edge is sewn by approximately 0.75 cm. Care should be taken to ensure the facing does not slip away and stays precisely at the edge.

Fixing the pocket opening

Picture 359

Next, the edge of the pocket opening is carefully basted, and the actual opening is marked. It's crucial that the fabric pattern aligns perfectly. The length of the pocket opening should be around 16 cm.
The edge of the opening can be fixed either by using the sewing machine or by hand.

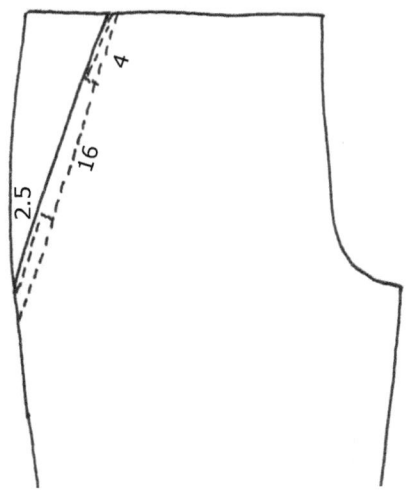

Remarking the side seam

Then, the side seam has to be re-marked. Either with the curve ruler, freehand, or simply by laying the pattern on top and re-tracing it.
The facing and the pocket bag are then basted together at the side seam. This ensures that nothing can slip when serging the side seam.

Serging the front

Picture 360

The overlock sewing machine can now secure the side seam, the fly, and the inside seam on the front trousers. On the back trousers, only the side seam and the crotch seam are overlocked. Alternatively, you can secure the edges with a zigzag stitch.
For preparing the back trousers' pockets, go to page 38.

When serging the trousers' parts, remember to overlock the rear edge of the fly's facing.

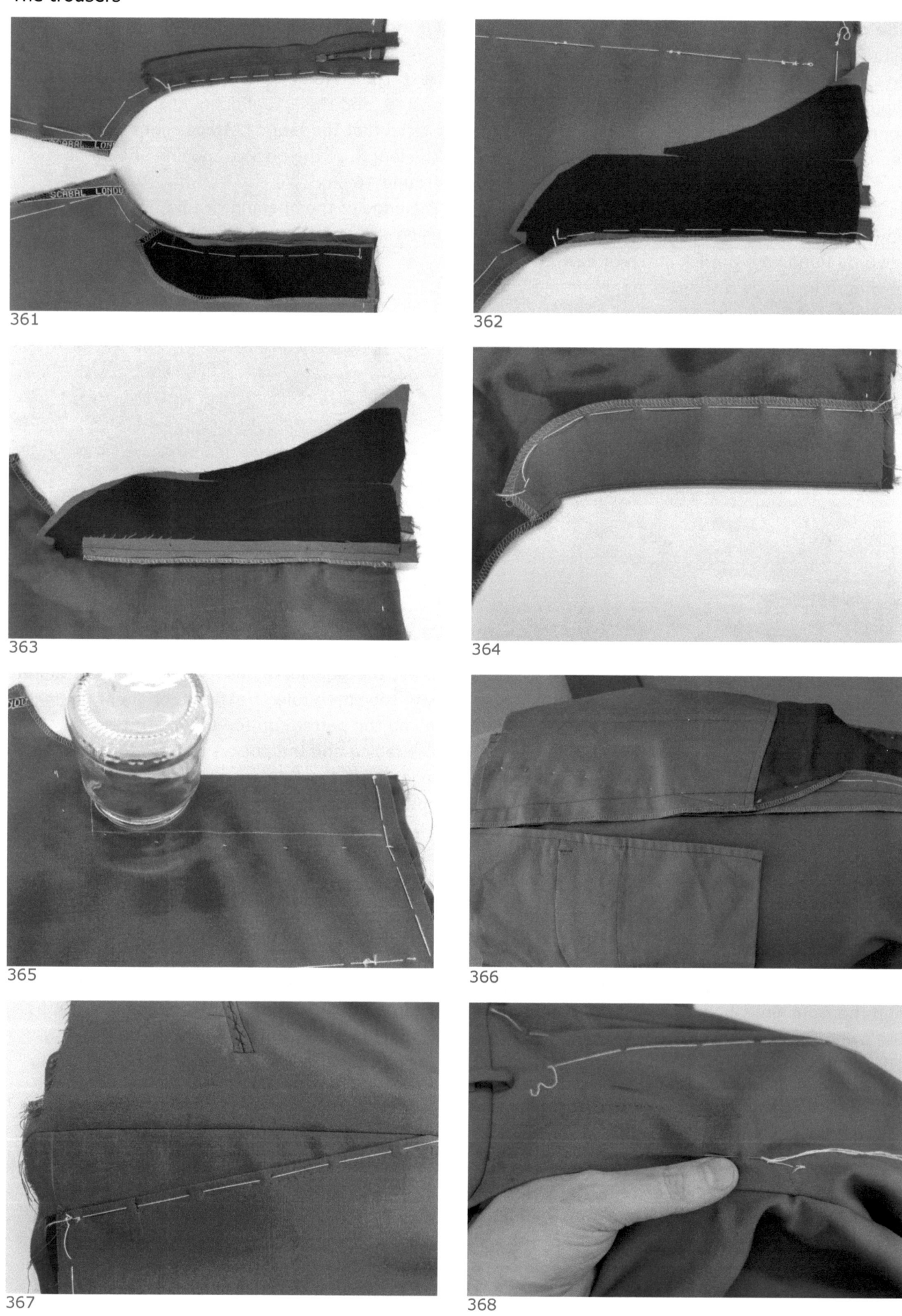

361

362

363

364

365

366

367

368

The right fly

Picture 361

First, the zipper is briefly ironed and tested to see whether it works properly.
Then, it can be pinned to the edge of the fly with minimal extra length.

Picture 362

Now, place the reinforced fly extension onto the zipper, attach it with minimal extra length (just a few millimetres) and mark the end of the seam.

Picture 363

Then, the seam is sewn, secured at the lower end and ironed open.

The left fly

Picture 364

The reinforced facing is attached to the left front part, and the end of the seam is marked. After sewing, the seam allowance is pinched at the seam's end, and the facing is turned over and sewn.

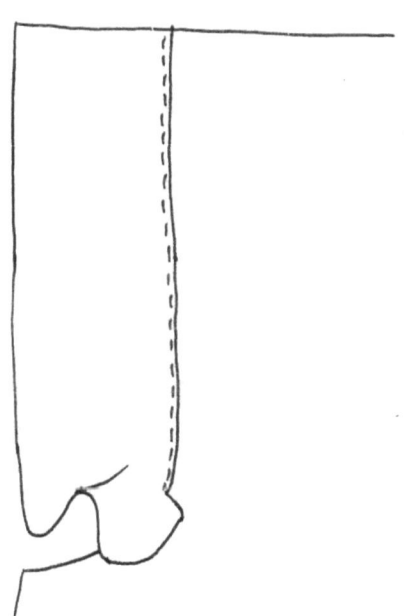

Then, the fly facing is turned over, ironed flat and basted.

Picture 365

A seam is marked by a width of approximately 3.5 - 4 cm, and a nice curve is drawn at the lower end. Then, fix the facing to the left front trousers. This seam can either be sewn by hand with a point stitch or by machine.

Closing the side seam

Place the back trousers onto the front trousers and fix them with pins. With a fabric pattern, the entire side seam must fit. Now the side seam is sewn with the sewing machine on the back trousers with 2 cm seam allowance (or as much as you left when cutting). Ensure that the fabric pattern does not slip away (see page 60).

Picture 366

First, check whether the seam runs evenly and the fabric pattern fits. Then, iron open the seam. Because of the hip arch, the upper part of the side seam should be pressed on the ironing pad. Here, the seam allowance should be ironed toward the back.

Picture 367

Then, the seam can be pressed carefully from the right side. Now follow the instructions on the pages 60-72.

The fly extension

The fly extension with a zipper is processed similarly to the fly extension with the button placket (See page 66 starting from picture 200).

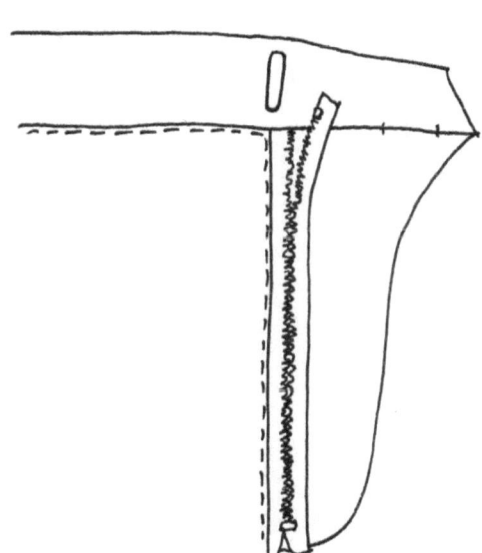

Attaching the zipper

Picture 368

After sewing the seat-seam, the fly is now placed together, so the zipper and seam are invisible. Then, the zipper is basted to the left front trousers' fly from the right side.

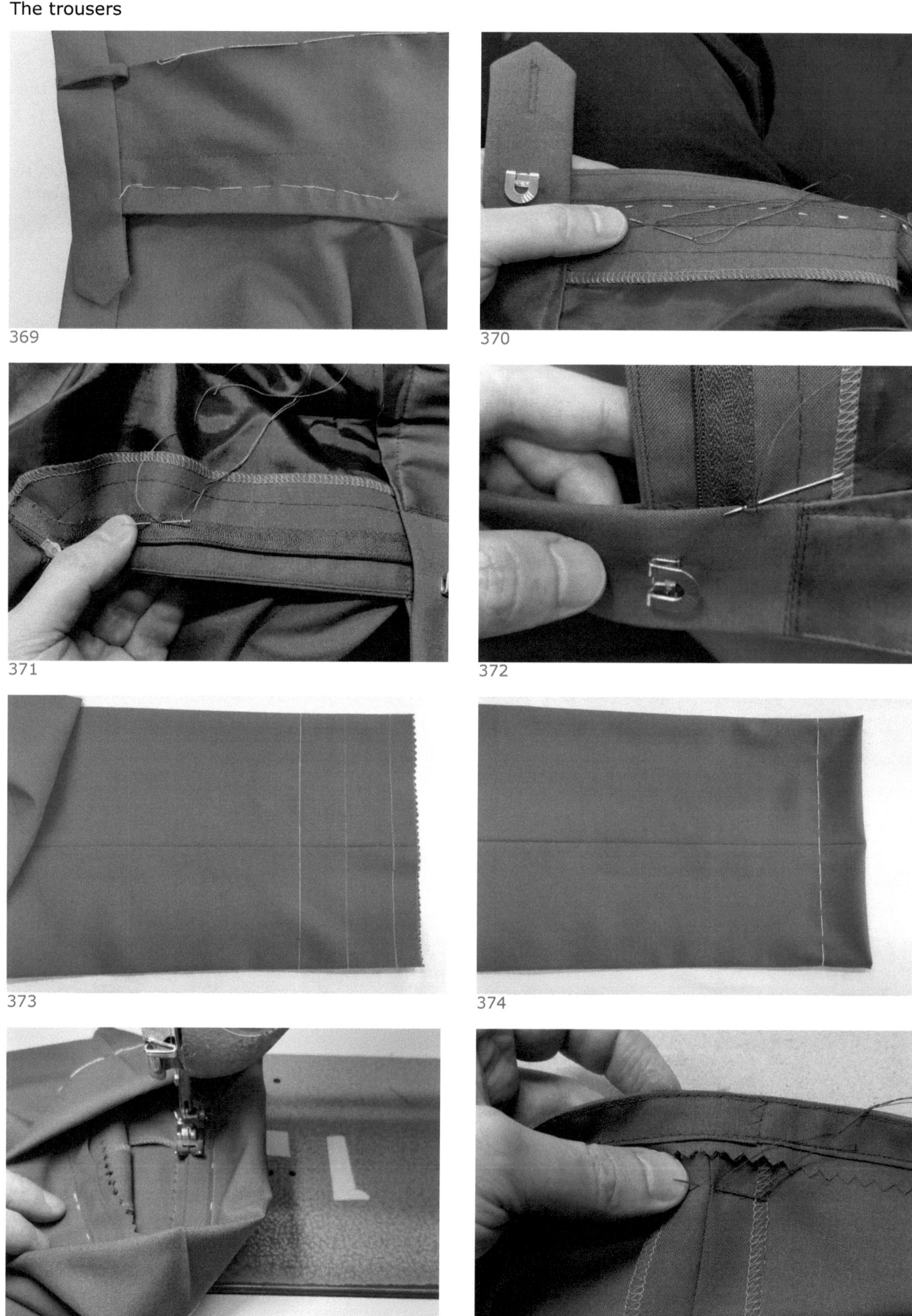

369

370

371

372

373

374

375

376

Picture 369

The zipper must not be stretched but should have very little fullness (a few millimetres). The end of the zipper is pushed into the open part at the waistband. (See image 371)

Picture 370

Then, the zipper is sewn in by hand using a blind stitch and buttonhole thread from bottom to top.

Picture 371

The zipper is secured with two seams. On the way back down, it is sewn with a prick stitch approximately 0.5 cm from the edge.

Picture 372

The short distance at the waistband, which is still open, is now sewn up with buttonhole thread using a blind stitch.

The turnup hem
Picture 373

From the length downward, the width of the turn-up is marked twice. As a spare, approximately 2 cm are marked; then, the trousers' legs are cut to size with pinking shears.

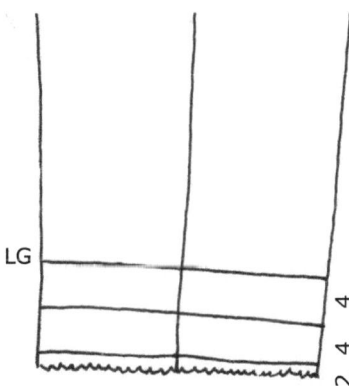

Picture 374

Now, the hem allowance is turned in, and the hem is basted evenly along its length. The chalk lines should match.

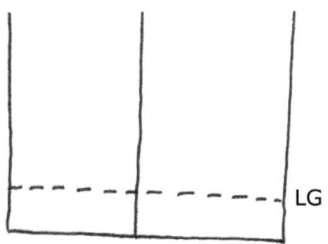

The kicktape

The 3 cm wide kicktape is now folded over by 0.75 cm on both sides, one after the other, and machine-stitched.

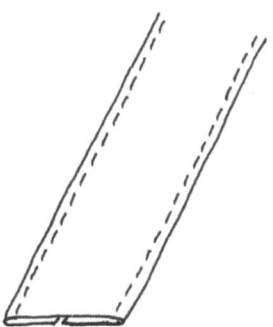

Alternatively, of course, a ready-made kicktape can be used. However, this will never fit perfectly in terms of colour and is mostly very stiff.

Picture 375

The kicktape is then sewn on above the chalk/baste line. With a turn-up, there is no need to turn the trouser leg inside out beforehand.

Picture 376

Now, remove all basting threads. Finally, the turn-up is folded upward, ironed flat, and fixed with hand stitches from the inside on both the inseam and the side seam.

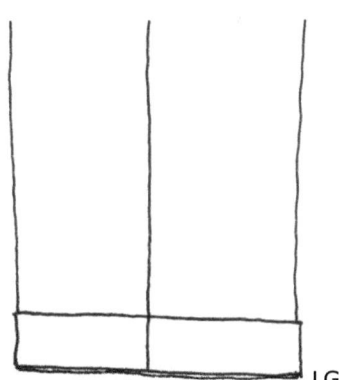

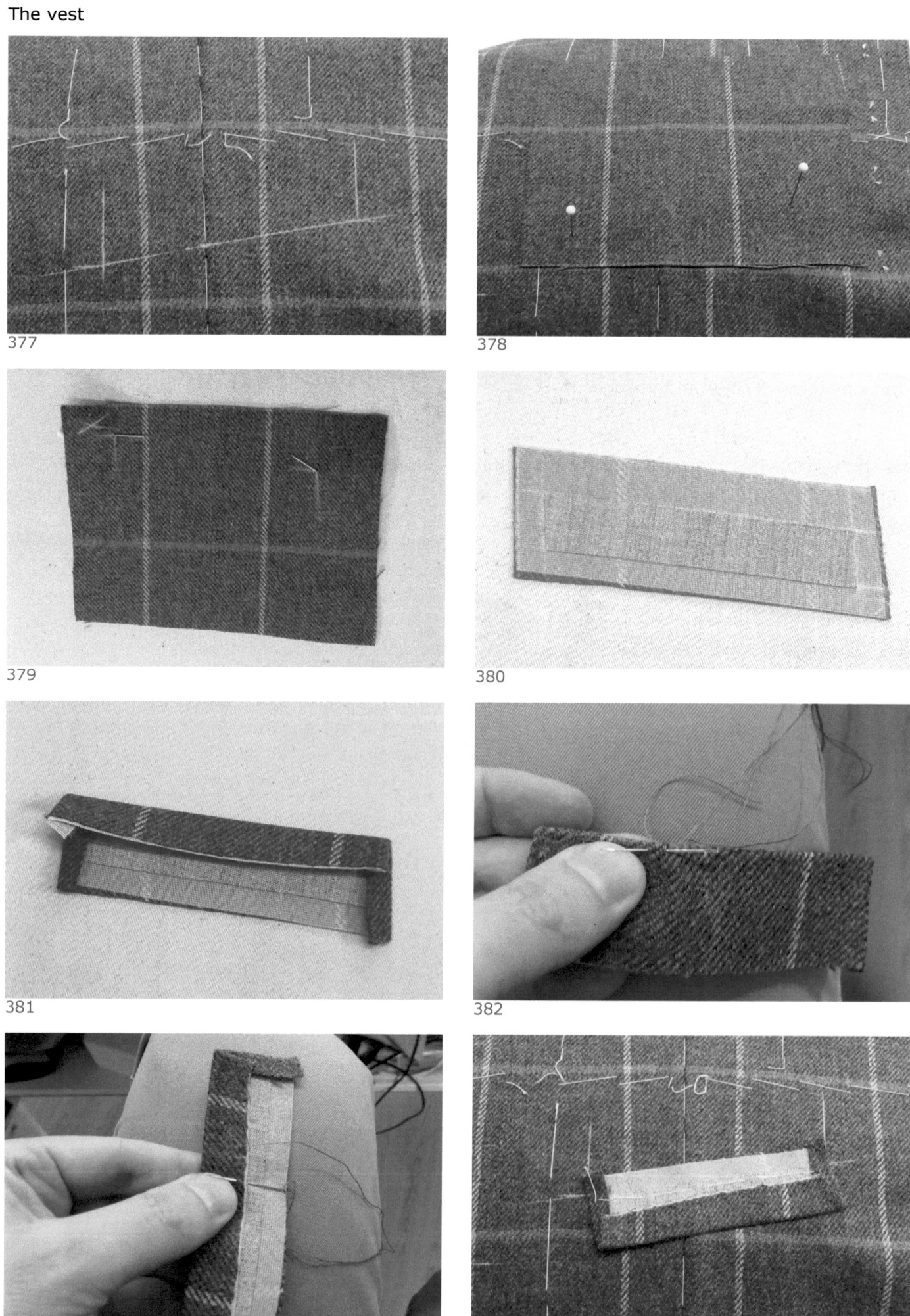

377

378

379

380

381

382

383

384

Marking the welted pockets

Picture 377

First, the pocket is marked at the correct position and transferred precisely to the other front part.

Marking the welt

Picture 378

Then, a spare piece of fabric is placed onto the pocket opening so the fabric pattern fits in front of the dart. Ideally, you make it easier for yourself while cutting by not necessarily having a horizontal stripe in the welt (checkered cloth). Of course, this only works with a large fabric pattern.

Now, pins are inserted precisely at the pocket opening's beginning and end. The fabric should not slip.

Picture 379

Then, the fabric and the needles are taken off. Ensure the needles do not slip out, and mark their positions on the back.

Inforcing the welt pocket

Picture 380

Now, the welt can be marked precisely.
A thin fusible interlining is ironed to the back and cut to size.

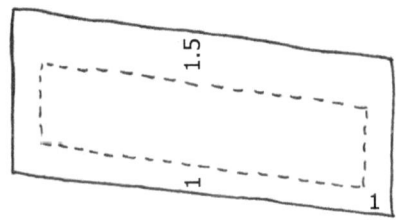

A piece of fusible horsehair is ironed to the back in the size of the finished welt.

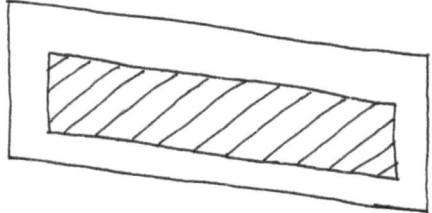

Picture 381

The welt is now folded and ironed flat at the sides and top.
Because of the angle, the seam allowance has to be cut away at the back corner; do not cut too close to the edge.

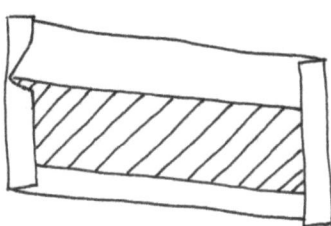

Using a pin can help to get the corners nicely pointed when ironing.

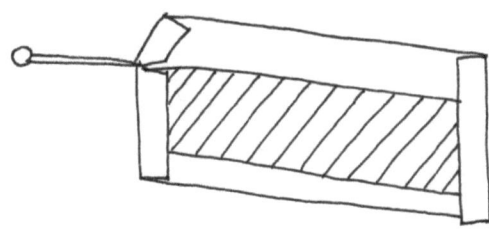

Picture 382

Now, the edge of the welt is hand-sewn with a sinking stitch.

Picture 383

The seam allowance is loosely attached to the horsehair.

Picture 384

The welt is now basted exactly into place according to the pattern. This requires a little practice, as the welt is basted by facing right sides to each other. So, you only see the final result after sewing. Do not be afraid to undo this seam if the result is inadequate, and retry.

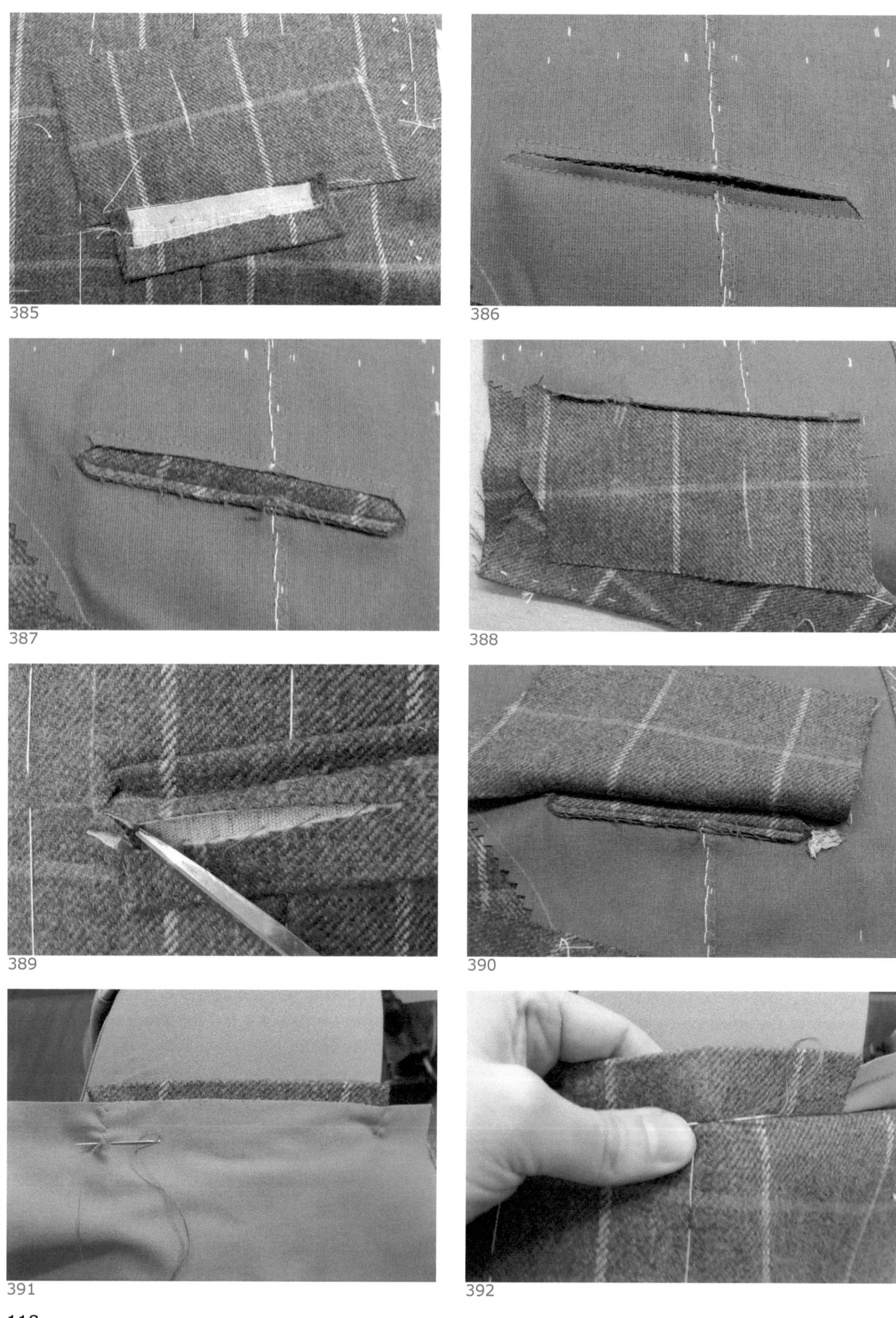

385

386

387

388

389

390

391

392

Attaching the welt

Picture 385

The pocket facing should be long enough to be used as a pocket bag.
The welt's beginning and end are marked on the facing and drawn 0.5 cm narrower on both ends.

Cut open the welted pocket

Picture

Then, the welt and the facing are sewn. The fabric pattern should be rechecked before cutting the pocket opening between the seams to ensure it matches precisely.

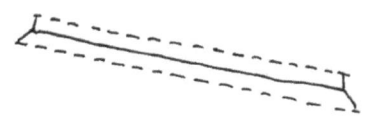

Picture 387

The front part is now held at the hem and pulled over the ironing pad. So, the welt is turned over, and the facing is still flat.
Then, the seam of the welt is ironed flat.

Picture 388

The facing is carefully pulled through the pocket opening, and the seam is ironed flat.

Securing the corners

Picture 389

At the front corner, the seam allowance at the welt is pinched but not cut away.

Picture 390

This corner is pushed inward through the pocket opening and sewn in place without piercing the outer fabric.

Attaching the pocket bag

Picture 391

Now, a pocket lining is sewn to the inside of the welt with a blind stitch approximately 1 cm below the edge.

Picture 392

The pocket lining is sewn with a prick stitch from the outside precisely in the seam shadow of the welt.

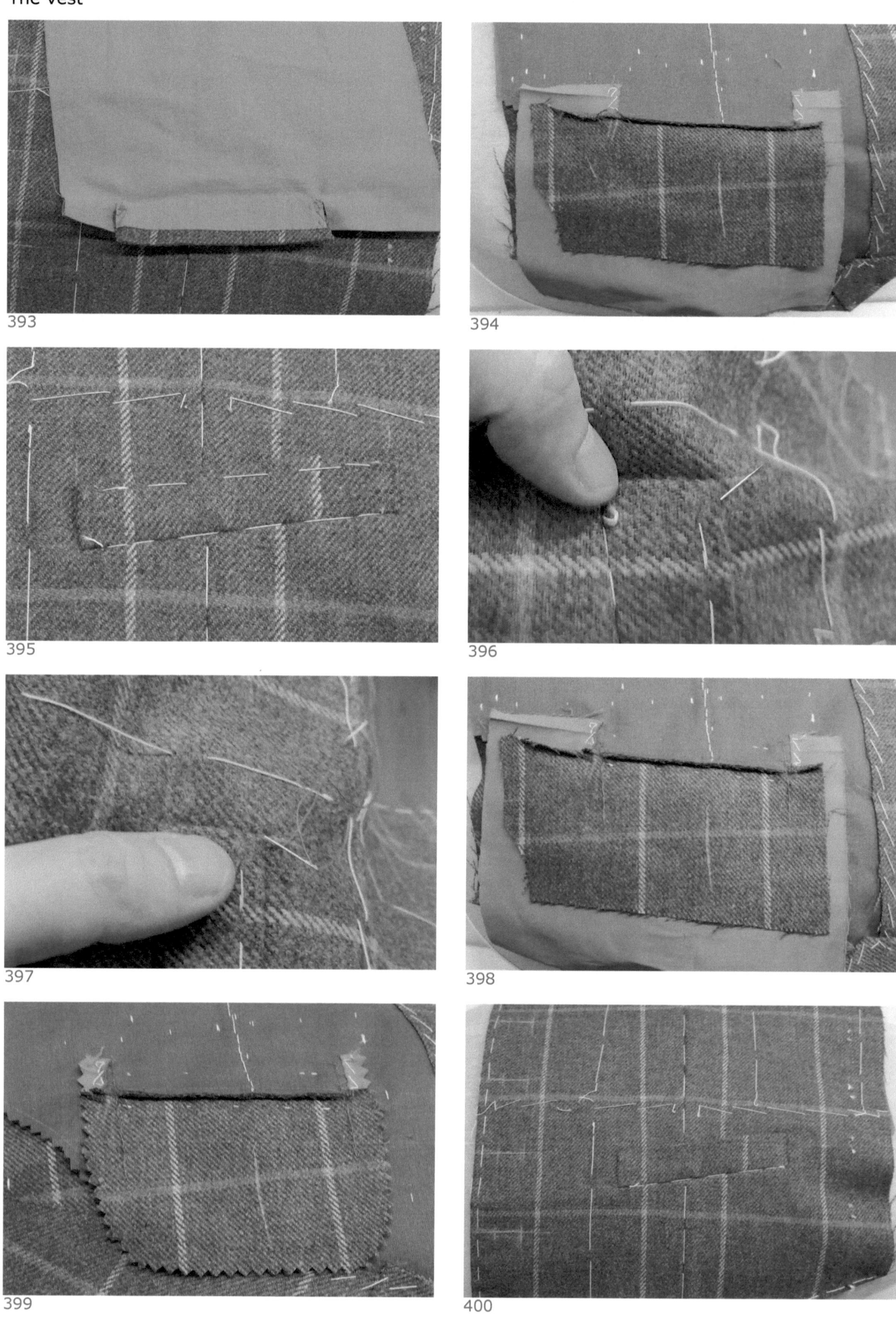

393

394

395

396

397

398

399

400

Attaching the pocket bag inside

Picture 393

The pocket lining is now cut at the beginning and end of the welt down to the seam.

Picture 394

Then the pocket lining is pushed in through the pocket opening and fixed with basting thread.

Closing the welted pocket

Picture 395

The welt is now basted exactly in the seam shadow and on the upper edge. The fabric pattern should fit exactly in front of the dart.

Fixing the welt

Pictures 396/397

Now, the welt is sewn at the sides with a small stitch. The needle is used to pierce up and down, and the thread is not pulled too tight. When piercing upward, the welt is only caught at the edge, and when piercing downward, the needle is inserted right next to the edge. You should still pay attention to the fabric pattern.

Picture 398

On the backside, the welt is secured a second time with a backstitch approximately 0.5 cm next to the edge. All layers will be connected, but you should not puncture the outer fabric. The hand seam goes down approximately 3 cm into the pocket bag so that it can be closed better with the sewing machine.

Closing the pocket bag

Picture 399

Finally, the pocket bag is closed and cut with pinking shears to ensure that the inside is not visible on the outer fabric after pressing.

Picture 400

The fabric pattern at the welt fits precisely into the pattern of the front part before the dart.
A dart must also be inserted in the welt if it has to disappear entirely in the fabric pattern.

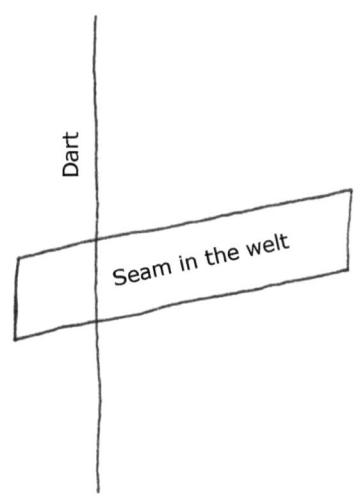

Dart

Seam in the welt

121

Pocket bag

Fold

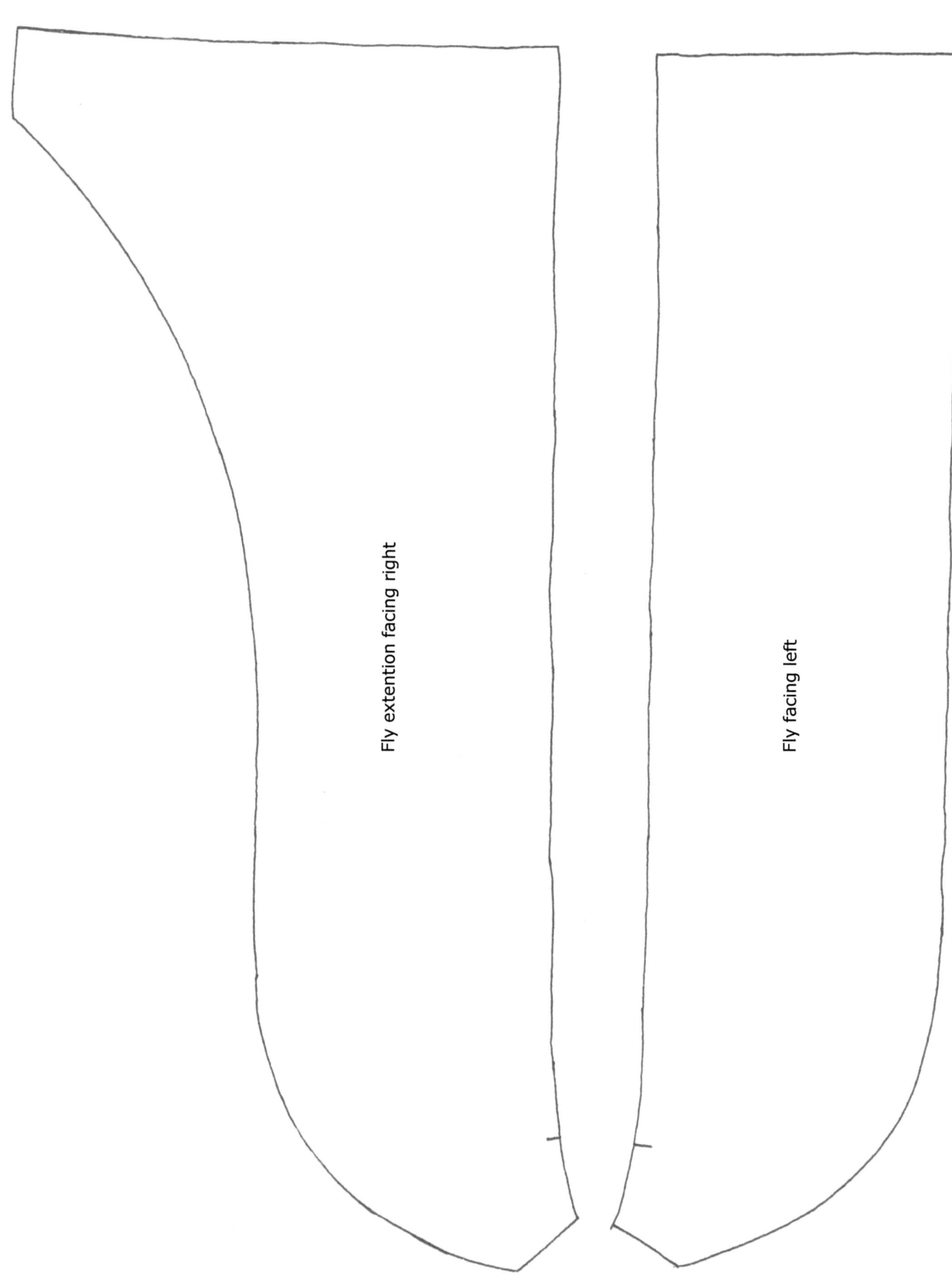

Fly extention facing right

Fly facing left

Sven Jungclaus

completed his training as a bespoke lady's and men's tailor in the 1990s with Heinz-Josef Radermacher in Dusseldorf. At that time, he worked for musical productions like *Grease* and *Forever Plaid* in Dusseldorf, as well as The Beauty and the Beast and *The Fearless Vampire Killers* in Stuttgart. After eight years at the *Bavarian State Opera* in Munich as a master tailor and head of men's costume, he has deepened his expertise at the *Royal Shakespeare Company* in Stratford upon Avon, the *Deutsche Oper am Rhein* in Dusseldorf and the *Salzburg Festival*.

From 2013 to 2023, he produced bespoke clothing for men and women in his tailor shop, Gewandmanufaktur, in Salzburg. In addition, the versatile tailor worked regularly for the costume workshop Das Gewand in Dusseldorf and was requested for operas or musical productions e. g., the Metropolitan Opera in New York, the Nasjonale Opera in Bergen, the Theater Basel, the Musical Chicago in Stuttgart and Berlin, Het Muziektheater in Amsterdam, the Salzburg Festival or the Theater of Nations in Moscow.
Since 2023, he has managed the costume department at the Salzburg State Theatre.

Another passion of Sven Jungclaus is Becomeatailor, an internet presence with professional tips on craft, patterns, processing instructions, and other know-how for many costume epochs.

www.becomeatailor.com

Link to the website

https://www.becomeatailor.com

Index

Index

Abbreviations

CF	Center front
LG	Length
WB	Waistband
WOL	Width of length

Seam width

The seam width is defined by the width of the sewing machine foot. It is the distance between the needle and the edge of the foot and depends on the type of sewing machine.
Traditionally, the seam width is 0.75 cm and is already included in the patterns, but with modern patterns, it can also be 1 cm.

Tex

This is the unit in which the thread strength is measured. Actually, it's more about the weight per 1000 meters, but that is what determines the thread strength. The higher the number, the thicker the thread. (1 tex = 1 gram per 1000 meters)

GUIDE TO MEN'S TAILORING

Volume II

How to tailor a jacket

Sven Jungclaus

The perfect fit in men's tailoring

Adjust your patterns easily

Jungclaus

Reprint from 1890
Just available in German

You will find information about the books and more on our website.

Supplier and manufacturer list

Tailoring supplies
Ditta piero Zamboni
Bologna, Italy
Phone: +39 051 392980
www.foderezamboni1948.com

Bernstein & Banleys Ltd.
Essex, United Kingdom
Phone: +44 1702 523315
www.theliningcompany.co.uk

Whaleys Ltd.
Bradford, England
Phone: +44 1274 576718
www.whaleys-bradford.ltd.uk

Buttons
Knopf Budke GmbH & Co. KG
Phone: +49 7262 91350
www.knopf-budke.de

Müllerknöpfe
Large selection of suit buttons.
(Minimum order quantities)
Vienna, Austria
Phone: +43 1 8042662
www.muellerknoepfe.at

Tailor stands and ironing pads
Ortner GmbH
Cheap tailor mannequins according to your
measurements. Great quality!
Offingen, Germany
Phone: +49 8224 7677
www.ortner-gmbh.de

Free pattern programm
Seamly 2D (also known as Valentina Project)
An open-source program that is constantly being
developed and works for all pattern systems.
With a large community and the opportunity to
realize your own wishes and ideas, or to program
yourself.
www.seamly.net
www.valentina-project.org

Fabrics
Acorn Fabrics (Cumbria) Ltd.
Mostly shirt fabrics
Nelson, United Kingdom
Phone: +44 1282 698662
www.acornfabrics.co.uk

Harrisons of Edinburgh
Cloth and linings
Exeter, England
Phone: +44 1392 822510
www.harrisonsofedinburgh.com

Irons and sewing machines
Sewtex webshop
They sell the italian steam iron "Vaporino Inox"
at the best price!
Phone: +49 381 12769083
www.sewtex.de

Hangers
Kleiderbügelfabrik Rudolf Weber KG
Bad König, Germany
Phone: +49 6063 93130
www.weber3000.de

Labels
DORTEX Werbung und Vertrieb mbH
Lots of options for a small price.
Dortmund, Germany
Phone: +49 231 9371000
www.dortex.de

Garment bags and more
Morplan Ltd.
Essex, England
Phone: +44 330 4455666
www.morplan.com

Cloth brushes
Bürstenhaus Redecker GmbH
Large selection of natural, hand made brushes.
Versmold, Germany
Phone: +49 5423 94640
www.redecker.de